FIRST
TIME
OUT

FIRST
TIME
OUT

Skills For Living Away From Home

Reva Camiel & Hila Michaelsen

Illustrated by Brian Duffy

JALMAR PRESS
Sacramento, California

Printed in the United States of America
Library of Congress Catalog Number 79-92821
ISBN: 0-915190-26-5

FOREWORD

This is the first book I have ever seen that puts so much together in so compact a way about the pitfalls and complexities of living. It gives practical information that can help to reduce the stress and point the way toward helpful solutions.

While it is geared toward the starting out on one's own, it will be helpful to almost anyone.

Virginia M. Satir

Author of *Peoplemaking,*
Making Contact, Self-Esteem,
and other books.

CONTENTS

I. INTRODUCTION

PREFACE

HOW THIS BOOK CAME ABOUT

The idea for this book was born at a professional meeting for family therapists. Walking in the shadow of the Maroon Bells, near Aspen, Colorado, we, Reva Camiel and Hila Michaelsen, talked about our work and our own families. Between us we are the parents of four young adults, three of whom have recently left home and one of whom is preparing to do so. It was true for both of us that as the time for leaving approached, our children began asking many questions—each question bringing new awareness, new information that they were storing for future use. We decided to combine our experiences and knowledge to create a book which could be helpful not only to our own children, but to all people facing the same situation.

One of our foremost responsibilities as parents has been to help our children become autonomous people. However, as departure time came, we wondered if we had prepared them to cope with the countless daily decisions and situations they would be encountering. Did they have the skills and tools to prosper on their own?

FIRST TIME OUT addresses the practical areas of living on one's own. We have included information and resources that we believe are relevant to young adults. Information of this kind may become dated, but this book offers a framework for thinking and decision making. We stress the need to ask questions, to do research, to become a good consumer, to reach and try to find answers.

Unique to this book is the Roots and Records section. Here, parents can give their child a record of his or her family, medical, educational, and religious history. This section is a valuable aid in working with a physician, in filling out lengthy application forms for either work or school, and in answering some of the inevitable questions that crop up later in life about our earlier history. In several other places in this book, there is an opportunity for parents to offer advice, remedies and information.

We see this book as a point of departure. A bibliography at the end of each section suggests other highly specialized books and resources which offer more information.

FIRST TIME OUT is our way of helping celebrate this new phase of growth and family life.

TO THE READER

After all the years you've been told not to write in books, it may be difficult to break the habit. But this is a book designed to be written in—in the blank spaces provided, in the margins and on the extra pages.

We have covered many areas of living that are bound to affect you as you leave your family, home and community. But be aware that specific information can go out of date very quickly. Our sections are written to help you know what questions to ask, what to look for and where to look. We would like to help you not to make assumptions but to check things out and remain open to new information and learning.

Your best resources for finding new and accurate information are in libraries and bookstores. Here you can find the most recent books and pamphlets with up-to-date facts. Government agencies, both federal and local, are also valuable sources. Even the telephone book can be a tool once you have taken the effort to learn how phone books are set up. (For city offices and agencies look under the name of the city; do the same for the county; for federal agencies look under the United States.)

Before you leave, sit down with your parents and go through the Roots and Records section. Try to fill in all the data. Also, flip to some of the other fill-in pages and get some time and money-saving tips from your parents. One of the goals of this book is to get you in the habit of keeping records. If you jot down the name and number of the nearest hospital emergency room before you need it, you won't be looking for it when you're under stress. Similarly, if you keep a record of major illnesses and other important medical information, it will save you time, possibly eliminate expensive tests and give your physician more accurate information about you.

It's our aim that FIRST TIME OUT will make your first time out a smoother and fun experience. Fill in the information and keep it handy for your own reference.

II. THE OUTER WORLD

MONEY MATTERS

Over the course of your working lifetime, many thousands of dollars, indeed maybe millions, will pass through your hands. However, this section is based upon the assumption that for the next few years your money will be tight, as you are completing your education or training. Your main concern will be making it through each month or year. You will probably need to follow a budget more stringently now than ever before or in the future. Even later, in order to meet long range goals, you will need to have and follow a sound financial plan.

Part of any budget plan includes savings. Financial counselors advise that no matter how small your income you should put some money into a savings account on a regular basis. Not only does this get you into the habit of saving, but the money saved can be a life-saver in an emergency. As your income grows you can start to think about saving and investing in ways that can really make the money work for you.

In this section, we show you how to design a money plan for yourself using a worksheet developed by the Bank of America. Included are two brief descriptions of ways to keep track of your money and bills. Checking and savings accounts are discussed, as are how you establish credit and use credit cards.

Your income, not your age, determines whether you pay taxes; we point out some important information on this subject. We conclude the section with some consumer information which is intended to help you to be a more knowledgeable consumer.

MANAGING YOUR MONEY

We know of no one so wealthy that he/she doesn't have to plan for major expenses; most of us make plans, that is, a budget, for even minor expenses. You've probably already been doing some budgeting although you perhaps didn't use that word. When you planned on using your summer earnings to pay for your yearbook, a lens for your camera or Christmas gifts, you were, in fact, budgeting your money. If you actually put money away to cover each of these items, you were following through on your budget plan. Now, whether you're going on to school or on to a job, you will have more opportunity and greater need to budget.

On the following pages you will find a Money Planner Work Sheet which was prepared by the Bank of America as part of their consumer education program. Take some time to study the MPWS and make adjustments for your current life situation. For instance, if you're a student living at home, you'll probably eliminate many of the housing costs but you'll need to break down the educational expenses in greater detail. If you're living in a dorm, you'll have room costs but you won't have to buy much furniture. If you're working in a hospital or restaurant, you may need to buy uniforms and you would then want to divide your clothing expenses between work-related and non-work-related clothes.

As you look over the MPWS fill in those items which have fixed fees using one colored pencil; use a differently-colored pencil for those items which can be changed. Also, note that some MPWS items are marked by an asterisk. These are expenses that don't come due on a monthly basis but for which money must be set aside monthly to cover costs. Some of these items, like auto insurance and license registration, have fixed fees. Others, like vacations or cosmetics, can be changed depending on what funds you have available.

The Money Box

One of the best methods to make your money plan work for you in a hassle-free way is to set up a box or drawer in which you have separate, marked envelopes for every category of expense, e.g. rent, dentist, utilities, etc. At the beginning of the month, or whenever you get your money, put the money you've budgeted into the appropriate envelope; when a payment is due, withdraw what you need from the envelope. It is wisest to keep only small amounts of cash in the envelopes. For larger amounts, it is safer to deposit the money in the bank and write a check. You can also set up an envelope system for receipts for your cash payments and checks.

The Ledger Budget-Keeper

Another method for keeping track of expenditures is to use a ledger or notebook. Each page is headed with a separate budgeted item and set up in the following way:

Clothing					Budgeted Amount: $400.00
Date	Item	Amount	Paid/Date	Balance Due	Balance
9/27	Red sweater	$37.45	9/27	0.0	$362.55

This kind of record keeping will keep you aware of your current balance at any point. It will also alert you to seasonal shifts in spending, e.g. you spend more at the laundromat in the spring and summer. As you plan next year's budget, you can integrate these realizations and make changes to incorporate them.

Where Does It All Go?

If, month after month, you are bothered by the question of where your money is going, then it's time to look for "leaks." Take a small notebook with

MONEY PLAN

NET INCOME

Sources_____ **Annual** $_____   **Monthly** $_____

_____ $_____ $_____

_____ $_____ $_____

_____ $_____ $_____

Total   **Total**

Annual $_____   **Monthly** $_____

EXPENSES	Annual		Monthly	
	Now	Goal	Now	Goal

HOUSING

Rent, Home Loan Payment	_____	_____	_____	_____
Property Taxes, Assessments*	_____	_____	_____	_____
Property Insurance (homeowner, tenant)*	_____	_____	_____	_____
Maintenance, Repairs*	_____	_____	_____	_____
Utilities	_____	_____	_____	_____
Gas, Electricity	_____	_____	_____	_____
Other Fuel	_____	_____	_____	_____
Telephone	_____	_____	_____	_____
Water, Sewer	_____	_____	_____	_____
Cable TV	_____	_____	_____	_____
Garbage Collection	_____	_____	_____	_____
Home Furnishings*	_____	_____	_____	_____
Other (such as homeowners' association dues, household help *other than* child care)	_____	_____	_____	_____

PERSONAL MAINTENANCE

Food	_____	_____	_____	_____
Clothing				
Purchases*	_____	_____	_____	_____
Laundry, Drycleaning,				
Repairs	_____	_____	_____	_____
Self-Improvement				
Education	_____	_____	_____	_____
Books, Magazines, Newspapers	_____	_____	_____	_____
Entertainment & Recreation Vacations*	_____	_____	_____	_____
Other (including movies, sports, restaurants, hobbies)	_____	_____	_____	_____

WORK SHEET

EXPENSES	Annual		Monthly	
	Now	Goal	Now	Goal
Transportation				
Gas, Oil				
Repairs, Maintenance*				
Parking, Tolls				
Auto Insurance*				
License, Registration*				
Gifts & Holiday Expenses (*other than* Christmas Club accounts)*				
Child/Dependent Care (including babysitters, nursery school fees, convalescent care)				
Health Care				
Health Insurance				
Doctors' Visits				
Prescriptions, Medicine				
Personal Care (including barber, hairdresser, cosmetics)*				

Work Sheet Continued On Page 14.

you everywhere, and note each expenditure—everything from the 5 cents you put in the parking meter, to the 25 cents you paid for a pack of gum, to the $3.50 for the Saturday night movie. This is an exhausting job, but if you stick to it rigorously for a few weeks, you can discover exactly where your money is going.

Once you find out what's going on, you will have to decide how to readjust your budget. You may realize that you didn't allow enough for small pleasures in entertainment and recreation, and should add more for this category. To free up some money, though, you also have to decide where to cut back, such as reducing long-distance phone calls.

Inflation

Keep alert to changes in the economy. If the current rate of inflation continues to rise, you will have to make some major readjustments in your budget. Next year's prices will undoubtedly go up, so plan ahead with this in mind.

WORK SHEET

EXPENSES	Annual		Monthly	
	Now	Goal	Now	Goal

OBLIGATIONS

Regular Payments to Others
(including alimony, child
support, other court-ordered payments)   _____ _____   _____ _____

Contributions & Dues
(voluntary, including those
deducted from your paycheck)   _____ _____   _____ _____

Debt Payments

   Installment Loan Payments
   (for vehicles, furniture, etc)   _____ _____   _____ _____

   Credit Card, Charge Accounts   _____ _____   _____ _____

SAVINGS & INVESTMENT

Short-Term Savings (including
Christmas Club, emergency fund)   _____ _____   _____ _____

Long-Term Savings (including
company or private pension)   _____ _____   _____ _____

Life Insurance   _____ _____   _____ _____

Investments (including
stocks, bonds, real estate)   _____ _____   _____ _____

*Set-aside account

Reprinted with permission from Bank of America NT & SA, 'Personal Money Planner', CONSUMER INFORMATION REPORT No. 14, Copyright, 1977

OPENING A BANK ACCOUNT

Whether you're working or in school, you need a reliable bank in which to place your money. Bank personnel also can help you manage your finances. Some people opt to use the same bank for their checking and savings accounts; you may decide, after some research, to use different banks for these two functions.

Banking is a competitive business. Banks want and need your business! Before opening any account, find out the services and costs at all of the banks in your area. They are not all the same. The less money you have, the more important it may be to choose a bank which offers services such as prepaid postage, free traveler's checks, an income tax consultant, student loan officers, personal finance counseling, conveniently-located offices, banking hours that fit with your schedule, etc.

Checking Accounts

Checking accounts are useful to cover routine expenses and provide you with ready cash. When you go to open a checking account, investigate whether the bank has any minimum balance requirements. Many banks have a cut-off figure below which they charge you a fee to keep the account open. Banks also can charge you a fee for handling or processing your checks; this fee is usually referred to as a "service charge" and is most commonly computed on a per check basis, e.g. 10 cents per check.

It is up to you to keep an accurate record of each check you write. In your check register, which the bank ordinarily supplies along with your checks, you subtract from the balance whenever you write a check and add-in whenever you deposit money in the account. Get into the habit of filling in the check register. Besides helping you keep track, it also forms a practically indisputable record of whom you paid and when. Depending on your memory to recall what you spent usually leads to an inaccurate balance and increases the likelihood of "bouncing" a check—expensive and embarrassing! "Bouncing" happens when the amount the check is for exceeds the amount in the account. The banking term for such an event is "funds insufficient." Banks charge anywhere from $3-5 for each bounced check and the party you wrote the check to will also charge a similar fee. You can see, then, that two bounced checks could cost you $20, plus embarrassment.

Each month your bank will send you a "monthly statement" along with the checks you wrote during that month. These checks, which have been paid out of your funds by the bank, are referred to as "cancelled." It is wise to keep cancelled checks as a record that payment has been made. The monthly statement gives you the opportunity to see that your figures and the bank's balance out. If they don't, you have to either accept the bank's version or track down the error in arithmetic. Although many people will simply take the bank's version as more reliable, accidents happen, and more than one person has discovered errors in the bank's calculations. Reviewing your monthly statement and checks can give you a good overall picture of your spending habits and can be used as an aid in future financial planning.

Monthly statements and checks should be among the papers you keep on file. They will be important—not only for the afore-mentioned records and financial planning—but to verify data or claims for taxes and/or loans.

Maintaining your checking account in good order has an additional benefit. Many banks will issue cards to clients whose accounts have never bounced checks or otherwise been mishandled. Such cards are not credit cards, but simply show that you have been a responsible banking customer and that your account is reliable. You may have noticed that many stores or businesses ask for a driver's license and credit card when a customer wants to pay for a purchase with a check. In many cases, such business establishments will accept a bank's check-cashing card as a second form of identification. For those of you who do not have major credit cards nor anticipate acquiring any in the near future, such bank cards may fill this need. See what your bank's policy is on issuing these cards.

Savings Accounts

Establishing a savings account is a great way to make your money work for you. Savings accounts differ primarily from checking accounts in that they offer "interest." Interest is a fixed percentage which the bank pays you for the use of your money. For instance, if you deposit $1,000 in a savings account at a bank which offers 6 percent interest per year, your account will hold $1,060 at the end of the first year.

There are many different kinds of savings accounts offered by many kinds of institutions, e.g. banks, credit unions and savings-and-loan institutions. Many of these accounts have special conditions. For example, some of the higher-yielding interest rates are available only if the savings are deposited for a certain period of time and are not withdrawn before that time. If the funds are withdrawn, substantial penalties can be applied. You will want to find the place which pays the highest interest and has the lowest penalty, if any, for early withdrawals. Look carefully and investigate thoroughly.

Financial counselors suggest that you take a percentage of your monthly income, even if it's quite small, and put it into a savings account. You should do this on a regular basis. If your savings account has over $500 you may want to think about putting that money into a long-term account that pays even higher interest.

A savings account establishes the fact that you have a banking relationship. This is to your advantage when you want to establish credit.

ESTABLISHING CREDIT

To some people, credit cards represent the devil on earth, and to others they can be life-savers in times of need. If you understand how credit systems operate you can become an intelligent credit user.

Since we are a society that operates more on credit than on cash, it is wise for you to start establishing a credit file as soon as you can. Applying for credit for the first time can leave you in a quandry if you have no credit file, no employment history of long standing and are perhaps new in a community. Having a checking or savings account in a local bank may be helpful in establishing you as a good credit risk. Getting credit for the first time is just the start; you actually establish credit, one creditor at a time, by repaying your debts as agreed.

Your credit file is opened for the first time when you are granted credit. Your file will be updated as you apply for, use and repay credit throughout your lifetime. Your file contains information on your stability, income, expenses, employment record, banking history, creditors, credit limits, and how you pay your bills. Basically, all creditors look for the same thing before extending credit: your willingness and ability to pay on your debts. To determine your credit-worthiness, any business can have access to your credit file. There are no secrets that you can hide in the credit business.

Credit Cards

There are different kinds of credit cards. Visa and Master Charge, for instance, are credit cards obtained through banks. There is a charge for these cards. Some gas companies, such as Exxon or Shell, and many department stores also extend credit. All potential creditors want to look at the following in particular: your income, the length of residence at one address, your history of paying bills, and your length of employment. Students with no guaranteed income may be granted credit providing that they have at least one credit-eligible parent and s/he also co-signs for the card. The bank helps to determine your credit limit, that is, the maximum amount that can be charged on the card. As your income and your credit-worthiness increase, so too does your credit limit.

The stores which accept credit cards pay a service charge for them directly to the bank. This service charge usually hovers between 3-5 percent.

When you make purchases on credit, you are not billed for those purchases until the end of the month. At that point, you have the choice of either paying the amount in full or paying a "minimum monthly balance due." If you pay the entire amount, then there is no charge to you for the use of the card. The trouble comes when you pay only the minimum amount due, which is computed as a fixed percentage of the whole bill. The amount which you do not pay is carried forward for another month, at which point you have the same options. Any leftover balance, however, gathers 1½ percent interest every month it goes unpaid. This accumulates to a whopping 18 percent per year. The lesson is simple: If you buy on credit make sure that you will have the money to pay in full within one or two months or you will wind up paying a hefty service charge.

American Express, Diners Club and Carte Blanche are known as travel or entertainment cards and generally require annual incomes of at least $12,000 before credit is extended. These cards charge an annual membership fee of approximately $25.00, and offer their holders a much higher credit limit. These cards also differ from bank cards in that they require monthly bills to be paid in full and on time, although the cardholder may be allowed to fall behind a month or two. The one exception to this rule is travel bills which may be paid off in installments, at 12 percent annual interest.

PAYING UNCLE SAM

In March and April of any year, it's not unusual to overhear people talking about W-2's, short or long forms, adjustments, and the virtues of 1040 over 1040 A. To better understand all the issues you'll need to get your hands on *Your Federal Income Tax, Publication 17,* which is published by the Department of the Treasury, Internal Revenue Service, Washington, D.C. 20224. This essential handbook is available free of charge at many federal offices, such as the Post Office.

What follows is a brief overview about taxes and how you can organize your records so that preparing your own return is easier. This is only an overview of an enormous and complicated field. Unless your finances are very complicated, it should not be too difficult to process your own forms. But you are, of course, advised to read wisely and consult experts for individual-ized attention if you need help.

Who Pays Taxes?

It is the amount of your income, not your age, which determines if you must file federal and state income tax returns. The amount requiring that you file changes from year to year, so check out what the current figure is. To give you a rough idea, the amount of income which required a single person under 65 to file a federal tax return in 1979 was $3,300.

Even if your income falls below the required amount for filing, you may want to file a tax return. Many of the monies that were withheld from your paychecks are returnable! These monies cannot be returned unless you file a statement showing that they are due you. Sometimes, this can add up to a tidy amount. Ordinarily, these types of returns are very straight-forward and easy to prepare. You can even do it ahead of time, since you won't be paying any taxes, and receive your refund as soon as possible.

Keep records so that you know what your income was. Gross, or total, income includes wages, tips, commissions, interest from your savings ac-counts, dividends from stocks, capital gains, pensions, alimony, and any money received from jury duty, gambling winnings, and unemployment compensation.

By January 31 of the current year, your employers for the previous year must send you a Wage and Tax Statement, known as a W-2 form. The W-2's show your total earnings for the year, along with the exact amounts withheld for taxes and other purposes. If you have moved, make sure your old em-ployers are aware of your new address.

What About Your Parents' Return?

No matter how much income you earn, your parents may still claim you as a "dependent" if the following are true:

1. They provide more than half your support and you are under 19, and

2. You are a full-time college student for at least five months of the year.

Even if your parents are claiming you as a dependent, you are still entitled to your own personal exemption.

Your Return

The IRS bases personal income tax on the gross income you received from January 1 to December 31 of the previous year. Besides meaning total, gross means the amount of earnings before any state, federal or other taxes were removed from your paychecks. The amount after these taxes, the amount that you actually received, is termed the net amount.

The IRS has devised tables which tell you how much tax you owe on your gross income. You simply look up the figure that you earned in the tables, and then find the tax which is computed for that figure. On the average, the more you earn, the more you pay.

There are also "tax brackets" which, in conjunction with your income, dictate how much tax you pay. For most of you first starting out, though, you will fall in the first income bracket and will not need to worry about figuring out this aspect.

You are allowed to make certain "deductions" and claim certain "exemptions." A deduction is an item which you can subtract from your income. An exemption is an amount which the government fixes, allowing you to deduct for individuals. For example, you are allowed to deduct a certain amount for yourself. If you also supported a sister or child, you would be allowed so much for them.

The list of deductions and exemptions which are permissible is quite long and beyond the scope of this book. You will have to research what you can legally claim on your return. The government has publications on this issue, and there are many books—some of them not too complicated—which treat the subject.

Deductions and exemptions serve to lower your income, since they are subtracted from your gross income figure. Of course, the lower your income becomes, the less taxes you are likely to pay. For instance, if your gross income were $4,000 and you had $400 in deductions, you would proceed to pay tax on $3,600. In this way, many people manage to get their incomes lowered. Sometimes the deductions may be so extensive as to eliminate the income tax altogether.

Record Keeping

You are responsible for proving that your records and claims are in order. If the IRS questions your figures, the burden is on you to prove their accuracy. If you don't have proof—cancelled checks, sales slips, receipts, statements of earnings—the IRS may disallow your claims. In some cases, if your claim is disallowed, you will have to not only pay penalties but pay the money you owe with interest.

Browse through a good stationery store and look at various income-tax organizers now on the market. You will find them in book, log, file, and envelope form. Some banks also offer materials to help keep your tax records organized. Purchasing one of these organizers makes it much easier to keep and record all the items of information you will need when you file your tax return.

How Long to Keep Records?

Keep records until the statute of limitations for the return expires. That is, three years from the date the return was filed or due, or two years from the date the tax was paid, whichever is later.

If you think your income may increase sharply in the next few years, hold copies of your previous tax returns and cancelled checks, etc. for at least five years. By doing so, you may also be eligible for income averaging which is a tax advantage to you. Investigate this possibility.

Tax Help

1. The IRS will help with advice and will even, under certain conditions, figure your tax for you. Call your local IRS office, or for information and assistance, call 800-772-2345.

2. Commercial tax services operate on a fee basis for their services, which depend on the complexity of the work. Ask the service what liability they will assume, that is, whether they will pay any penalties and interest if they make mistakes on your return. To find out the fee, go to the preparer's office with all your documents, or call and ask for a general estimate. Listings for these services are in the Yellow Pages under "Tax Preparation" or "Tax Return Preparation." You'll also notice ads on TV and in the newspapers for income tax services as D-Day , April 15, approaches.

3. Accountants are trained, and in some states licensed, professionals. A certified public accountant (CPA) can prepare your tax

return, advise you about money management and represent you in IRS audits and tax courts. Discuss your situation and ask for a fee estimate.

4. Enrolled agents are persons who have passed an exam given by the U.S. Department of the Treasury. Enrolled agents can prepare your tax returns and represent you to the IRS. There is a fee for this service.

One last word if you decide to use a professional in filing your return: Shop around. Fees will vary, as will quality. Find a reputable firm or individual within your price range.

Getting Your Money's Worth

Retailers are interested in your repeat business! They know that it is to their advantage to sell merchandise or services that work, or to help you, the consumer, by exchanging or refunding your money on defective products.

Unless stated in the contract of sale or posted in the store, you, the consumer, should understand that a refund is a privilege and not an absolute right.

Before buying major items such as a car, a TV or stereo system, or contracting for major services such as auto repair, do the following:

1. Read "Consumer Report" and/or "Consumer Research." These are publications of private research organizations and are available at public libraries and for purchase at newsstands. These periodicals are a great aid in pointing out what features to look for in each piece of equipment. Their rating scale of a wide number of national brands for each item is very helpful.

2. Shop around! Compare prices, service warranties, charge plans, and interest charges. All manufacturers and stores do not offer the same guarantees.

If the product you buy is defective—and you've checked to see that you've used it as directed—don't hesitate to take your complaint directly to the department supervisor or store manager. Some complaints can be remedied on the spot by giving you an exchange or your money back; other complaints have to go to "the head office" and may take weeks to resolve.

If you have trouble getting through to the top, send a letter by registered mail. The recipient must sign that the letter was received and, thus, you are assured they can't say your letter of complaint was never received. Always keep at least one copy of your letter along with the original sales tag, warranty and sales contract. If you need to send proof of purchase, make sure you send a photocopy (easily and inexpensively done at a copy machine found in libraries, large supermarkets, etc.) and hold on to the original. If, after two or three weeks, you have no satisfactory response from the company, call the nearest office of the Department of Consumer Affairs. The staff will advise you on how to continue pressing your complaint.

Learning to be a good consumer takes skill and information and energy. No one is born with such skills, but they can be acquired! The following information may be of help to you.

Door-to-Door Sales: Buyers of merchandise worth more than $25 may cancel the purchase within three business days.

Mail-Order Merchandise: Anything ordered must be shipped within 30 days unless a longer time is specified by the company.

Unordered Merchandise: If you receive unordered merchandise in the mail you may keep it. You are under no obligation to pay for it or to return it. Letters billing you for the merchandise are illegal and may be ignored.

Debt Collection: It is illegal for a debt collector to engage in abusive or deceptive acts in trying to collect on a debt. Violators should be reported to your local state office of consumer affairs.

Airline Passengers: If your flight has been overbooked, the airline must get you on another flight—within 2 hours nationally, within 4 hours on international flights—or provide certain amenities (hotel room, meals, ground transportation, and a long distance phone call) or reimbursement. You will have to ask what the exact ruling is for each case. The following resources are of help to the consumer.

1. The local Department of Consumer Affairs. The name of this agency may be different in your state—look in the telephone directory under "state agencies." Local offices usually have a helpful staff, plus numerous pamphlets, fact sheets, and other consumer information aimed toward helping you become a more alert consumer.

2. "Help: The Useful Almanac" 1978–79 ($4.95). This handy book can be found in libraries and has all the names, addresses and phone

numbers of non-governmental agencies that help with consumer problems.

Federal Consumer Agencies

1. Consumer Product Safety Commission
   Sets and enforces mandatory safety standards on products used in and around the home.
       Toll-free hotline for inquiries: (800) 638-2666

2. Food and Drug Administration
   Responsible for the purity and safety of food, drugs and cosmetics.
       Consumer Inquiry Section
       Food and Drug Administration
       5600 Fishers Lane
       Rockville, Md., 20852
           (301) 443-3170

3. Federal Trade Commission
   The FTC enforces anti-trust laws and a wide variety of consumer protection statutes including those related to credit, warranties and false advertising.
       Bureau of Consumer Protection
       Federal Trade Commission
       Washington, D.C. 20850
           (202) 523-3727

4. National Highway Traffic Safety Administration
   This agency writes and enforces safety standards which set minimum performance level on almost all forms of vehicles.
       Toll-free hotline: (800) 424-9393

5. Interstate Commerce Commission
   The area of ICC activity that affects most consumers is household moving on an interstate level.
       Toll-free hotline: (800) 424-9312 (Florida (800) 432-4537)

6. Consumer Information Center
   Serves as a distribution outlet for federal publications on a wide variety of subjects. Catalog of publications available four times per year at no charge.

Consumer Information Center
Pueblo, Colorado, 81009

7. U.S. Postal Service
Anything ordered through or sent through the mail
Postal Inspector in your town.

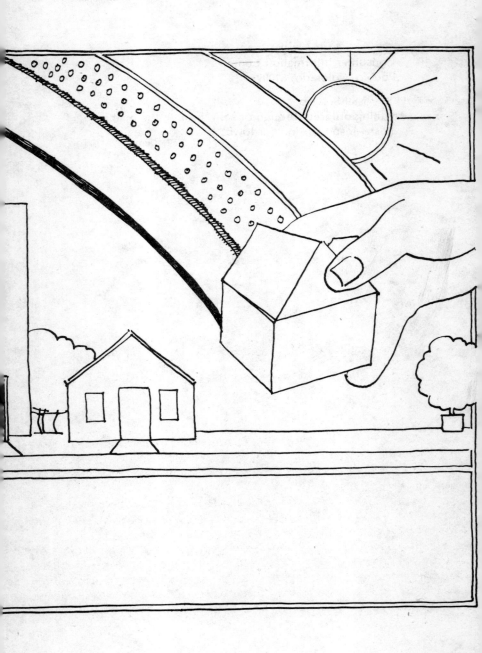

HOUSING

"He Huffed and He Puffed and He Blew the House Down"

Before you move to your new community, it's wise to do some thinking about where and how and with whom you are going to live. This chapter points out the different options and helps you to ask questions as to what fits best for you at this time.

Keeping track of all the places you look at can become a mass of confusion, but you will have a complete overview of where you have been and what you have seen if you use the Housing Search form.

If you decide to rent a house or an apartment, you will want to take care in signing a lease. We have included a sample rental agreement which is an excellent model to protect both you, the tenant and the landlord. You will also find an inventory checklist so that you and your landlord both agree on the condition of the rental at the time you move in.

The comfort you feel in the place you live affects your well-being and your performance at school or at work. Giving thought to the issues raised in this section will increase your chances of making a housing choice which works well for you. If it turns out that you are not satisfied with your choice, perhaps a review of this section will be an aid in selecting a new living arrangement.

WHAT TO LOOK FOR AND WHERE

In choosing a place to live, you'll want to consider many factors, including cost, convenience, transportation, and safety. Be aware of your needs. For example, do you function well with noise, or do you need quiet? Do you feel best in a sunny place? Do you thrive in a crowd, or love privacy? Do you like roughing it? Do you crave comfort?

To find an apartment or house that you share with others may sound like the best of all possible worlds. But take care before you jump into this! It's not unusual to find that despite how much fun you might have with another person, his or her living style might not be compatible with yours. Shared living space can become a battleground. Your dream house may have so many plumbing (or electrical, or roofing) disorders that you become more skilled at plumbing than you have time for.

Be aware of your transportation needs. Will it be safe and easy to travel to work, to the campus, to the grocery store, and the laundromat? Think about your time needs and whether you're going to be able to fit in shopping, cooking and cleaning. Financial experts advise that housing costs not exceed 25 percent of our monthly budget. How far off from this figure is the living situation you're looking at? Ask yourself these hard questions and others that will come to you, and remember, while the choice you make is important, it is not irrevocable. You may choose one kind of living situation for now, but others will be available at another time.

Aside from a dormitory and shared apartment or house, there are other ways you may choose to live:

a. Boarding house—meals may be communal or on your own

b. Fraternity or Sorority House—kitchen staff makes meals

c. Cooperative House—cooperative efforts in meals and upkeep

d. House with one room for rent—meals may be with one family or not; may include baby sitting, gardening or housework as part of payment

e. House sitting—care for pets and plants when owner is away (opportunities during summers)

f. Special interest house, i.e., only French is spoken, vegetarian, religiously oriented, etc.

g. Trailer

Sources of information that will help you locate housing:
Campus office (non-students can check here too)
Real Estate Agencies (listed in phone book)
Newspaper ads, Bulletin boards in schools and stores

Housing Check List

Look for a place that fits the kind of person you are:

☐ I need a building that provides security for its tenants.

☐ I want locked entranceways, announcing systems and a guard.

☐ I like an apartment where I can turn up stereo loud. I don't mind hearing my neighbors entertaining.

☐ I like to be close to public transportation.

☐ I don't like living upstairs.

☐ I need lots of closet space.

☐ I have a lot of things to store. I need storage space.

☐ I need a closed garage for my car.

☐ I like living alone.

Other things I want in a rental: _____

_____
_____
_____
_____

HOUSING SEARCH

| | Date | | Contact | | Type of | Result of |
$/Mo	Avail.	Comments	Address	Person	Phone	Housing	Contact
1. $120	9/1/	GL NS SU WD	141 Easy St.	Phil	981-2732	Upstairs apt.	Call back
2.							
3.							
4.							
5.							
6.							
7.							
8.							
9.							
10.							

Walt Whitman

GL - Good Location	**NS** - no smoking	**PF** - Partly Furnished	**V** - Vegetarian	**D** - Deposit req.
BL - Bad location	**F** - Furnished	**G** - Garage	**SU** - Share Util.	**WD** - Washer/Dryer
S - Smoking allowed	**UF** - Unfurnished	**Y** - Yard	**UI** - Utilities Inc.	

The authors wish to thank Daniel Green for developing this form.

FIX-IT TOOLS

In most dormitories, apartments and boarding houses, there is a manager or custodian who is responsible for major repairs and upkeep. Learn who that person is and put his/her name and telephone number in your personal phone book.

The more you know about minor fix-it jobs—changing a washer on a leaky faucet, unclogging a toilet, location of the fuse box and how to operate it—the less you will be dependent on someone else to take care of irritating tasks. These are not difficult skills to learn, and it has been our experience that salespeople in good hardware stores take special delight in teaching customers how to do each task. There are also good "fix-it-yourself" manuals that are a worthwhile investment.

You'll need some basic tools:

☐ Tool box large enough for equipment

☐ Hammer

☐ Pliers

☐ Drill (hand or electric)

☐ Wrench

☐ Phillips Head Screw Driver

☐ Measuring tape/ruler

☐ Plunger

☐ Awl

☐ Gimlet

☐ Brads (nails in various sizes)

☐ 3-in-1 oil

☐ Extension cord

☐ Flashlight

THE RENTAL AGREEMENT

There are three types of rental agreements:

1. An oral agreement: While an oral agreement is legal it offers little protection to either tenant or landlord when/if disagreements arise.

2. A written agreement: A written agreement lists the conditions (no pets, no sub-letting, etc.) and the obligations (date rent is due, upkeep of property, etc.). Usually written agreements run month-

to-month, which means you are not tied into a lease, but it also means you have no guarantee that you won't be asked to leave and/or that the rent will be raised.

3. A lease: Generally, a lease has the same conditions and obligations found in the written agreement. Additionally, a lease usually covers a year during which the rent cannot be raised and the tenant cannot be asked to leave unless one of the conditions or obligations is not met.

No matter which type of rental agreement you are offered, make sure it is spelled out clearly who is responsible for payments on which utilities.

If you don't understand any part of the rental agreement, don't sign it! There are books in the public library which are good resources for understanding legal jargon and other resources include the Board of Realtors, the Legal Aid Office, or a private attorney.

Tenant's Responsibilities

1. To pay the rent on the agreed upon date.

2. To keep the rental in about the same condition as it was when you moved in (i.e. the same, less wear and tear).

3. Under an oral or written rental agreement, you must give 30 days notice in advance if you want to leave. If you move without having given prior notice, you are liable for another month's rent.

Landlord's Responsibilities

1. To keep the rental safe, sanitary and liveable. Exact standards will vary according to state and municipality.

2. To make repairs within a reasonable time.

Eviction

The only legal way for a landlord to evict a tenant is to sue in a special lawsuit called "unlawful detainer." A landlord cannot call the police, physically threaten you, harass you, shut off your utilities or lock you out. If a landlord does—or threatens to do—any of the above, call an attorney immediately! Eviction is a complicated legal process. To know the exact ins and outs of the eviction process, call the Legal Aid Society, a large real estate office which handles rentals, or a rental-mediation service if there is one in your community.

RENTAL AGREEMENT

CAUTION: This is a legally binding agreement. **READ IT CAREFULLY.** It is intended to help promote harmony by clarifying the rights, duties, and responsibilities of property owners, managers, and renters. It may be added to or deleted from by having all parties initial each change.

Verbal agreements often lead to misunderstanding and confusion. MAKE SURE THAT ALL AGREEMENTS ARE MADE IN WRITING.

Both the Owner and the Renter(s) agree to fulfill the conditions listed below:
The OWNER IS:_____

The RENTER(S) is/are:_____
_____

ADDRESS of the RENTAL:_____

1. RENT
Rent shall be $_____per month, payable in advance on the _____ day of each month. Rent includes the following: (check each item included)

_____ Gas	_____ Trash Removal
_____ Electric	_____ Garbage
_____ Water	_____ Cable T.V.
_____ Parking	_____ Furnishings
_____ Range	_____ Refrigerator

_____Other (Specify)_____
_____

The Renter(s) will pay rent to the Owner or_____
_____

at the following address:_____
_____

or_____

2. FAILURE TO PAY RENT
If rent is not paid within (5) days after due date, the Renter agrees to pay a charge of $_____ (not more than one day's rent) for late rent and/or each dishonored bank check, unless waived by written agreement.
If the Renter is unable to Pay rent when due, the Owner has the legal right to serve notice to pay rent or vacate within three (3) days, as provided by California Code of Civil Procedures Section 1161.

3. OCCUPANCY AND SUBLETTING
A) The rental is for the residential use of the signers of this Agreement and is limited to_____adults and_____children?.
B) The Renter(s) will not sublet, assign, share or rent space, or maintain guests beyond_____days without the prior written consent of the Owner.

C) This Agreement is between the Owner/Agent and each renter individually. IN THE EVENT OF DEFAULT BY ANY ONE SIGNER, EACH AND EVERY REMAINING SIGNER SHALL BE RESPONSIBLE FOR ALL PROVISIONS OF THIS AGREEMENT.

4. PERMITTED ITEMS

Renter(s) may have the following items on the property

Animals_____

Waterbed(s)_____

Vehicles_____

All vehicles are to be parked in the following designated areas:

_____

_____

5. DEPOSITS

The Renter shall pay the Owner the following deposit:

$_____ REFUNDABLE CLEANING AND SECURITY DEPOSIT

A) When the Renter moves out the Owner may use the deposit for the purpose of:

    1) Repairing damages for which the Renter is responsible.

    2) Cleaning beyond normal wear and tear.

    3) Paying unpaid rent.

B) Check one

☐ The Owner shall place the deposit in a savings account and credit _____% interest compounded annually to the deposit.

☐ The Renter(s) shall not be entitled to any interest on the deposit.

C) The owners and the Renter shall inspect the rental BEFORE the Renter moves out at which time the Owner shall inform the Renter of needed repairs. Within two weeks after the Tenant moves out, the Owner shall return the deposit to the Renter with accrued interest, if any, less any deductions the Owner is entitled to under this Agreement. If any deductions are made, the Owner shall provide the Renter with a written itemized statement of expenses.

Renters with pets shall pay the Owner an additional deposit of:

$_____ REFUNDABLE PET DEPOSIT

6. MAINTENANCE OF THE RENTAL PROPERTY

A) COST

The cost of repairing or replacing items damaged beyond normal wear and tear will be paid by the Owner/Agent or Renter who willfully or through lack of due care caused or permitted the damage.

B) OWNER'S DUTIES

The owner shall keep the rental property tenantable, safe, and sanitary and in compliance with all state and local housing, building, and health requirements APPLICABLE to the rental property; shall have all required inspections and certifications, if any, made; shall maintain the mechanical equipment and utilities in good operating condition; and shall maintain the following in good repair and clean condition:

    1. Effective waterproofing and weather protection of room and exterior walls including windows and doors;

    2. Plumbing fixtures;

    3. A water supply capable of producing hot and cold running water, furnished to appropriate fixtures and connected to sewage disposal system approved under applicable law;

    4. Adequate heating facilities;

    5. Electrical lighting.

    6. Clean and sanitary building, grounds and appurtenances, free from all accumulations of debris filth, rubbish, garbage, and infestation by rats, rodents, and vermin;

7. An adequate number of appropriate receptacles for garbage and rubbish; and

8. Floors, stairways and railings.

The Owner further agrees to maintain peace and quiet in those areas of the building(s) not subject to the Renter's control.

C) RENTER'S DUTIES
Renter(s) shall:

1. Keep the premises as clean and sanitary as the condition of the premises permits;

2. Regularly dispose of all rubbish, garbage, and other waste in a clean and sanitary manner;

3. Properly use and operate all electrical, gas, and plumbing and fixtures and keep them as clean and sanitary as their condition permits;

4. Not, nor permit anyone on the premises within her/his control to, willfully or wantonly destroy, deface, damage, impair, alter, or remove any part of the structure, facilities, or equipment;

5. Leave the rental in the same condition as when possession was given to her/him, reasonable use, wear, and damage beyond the control of the Renter(s) excepted; and

6. Not make any excessive noise such as will disturb the peace and quiet of neighbors.

D) ADDITIONAL DUTIES
The maintenance of the following additional items shall be the responsibility of the Renter(s):_____

_____

_____

E) DESTRUCTION OF THE RENTAL
If the rental becomes partially or totally destroyed during the term of this Agreement, either party may thereupon terminate this agreement upon reasonable notice.

F) INSPECTION
The Renter(s) will permit the Owner or his/her agents, upon reasonable notice, to enter the rental between 8 a.m. and 6 p.m. to inspect, redecorate, clean, or repair the premises or to show the rental to prospective renters, purchasers, or representatives of lending institutions (24 hours is presumed to be reasonable by law). Such entries shall take place only with consent of the Renter, which consent shall not be unreasonably withheld.

If the Owner or his agent reasonably believes that an emergency (such as fire) exists which requires an immediate entry, such entry may be made without the Renter's consent. If such emergency entry occurs, Owner shall, within two (2) days thereafter, notify the Renter in writing of the date, time, and purpose of such entry.

G) RETALIATION RESTRICTIONS
In compliance with the law, the Owner may not reduce or terminate any services to the Renter, raise the rent, or evict the Renter if the Owner's purpose is retaliation against the Renter for seeking the following legal remedies:

1. Repair and Deduct.
   The Renter shall give a dated written notice (duplicated) to the Owner to repair or correct defects which are the Owner's responsibility as listed in subparagraph (B) above. After a reasonable time (generally 30 days), if the Renter has fulfilled her/his duties under the law, she/he may repair uncorrected defects or have them repaired and deduct the cost of repair from her/his next month's rent. Repairs must be made in a competent manner at reasonable cost, and the deduction cannot exceed one month's rent for each 12 month period as provided by California Civil Code Section 1942.

2. Reporting Code Violations:
   The Renter may report housing, building, or health and safety code violations to the City or County Building Inspection Department, the County Environmental Health Department, and/or other governmental authorities.

7. NOTICES

Notices and requests shall be made IN WRITING and given to the Owner at the Owner's address or place designated by Owner and to the Renter at the rental property.

RENT NOTICES

The Renter shall be given written notice of rent changes not less than thirty (30) days in advance of the day the rent is due.

VACATE NOTICES

Both Renter and Owner shall give thirty (30) days written notice in the event that the rental is to be vacated. This notice period may be lengthened or shortened by written agreement. (Less than 7 days notice to vacate is prohibited by California Civil Code Section 1946).

REPAIR NOTICES

A) Renter shall make a written request for repairs within five (5) business days of the problem's occurrence.
B) Renter's written requests for repairs shall be acknowledged by the Owner within five (5) business days of receipt.

OTHER CHANGES

The Owner shall give written notice within ten (10) days of any change in managers, agents for receipt of rent, and owners (or agents authorized to act for the owner). Such notices shall include the names, addresses, and phone numbers of such persons.

CAUTION: Verbal agreements often lead to misunderstanding, so GET IT IN WRITING.

8. DISPUTES AND REMEDIES

If a dispute occurs relating to the rental of this property, either the Owner or the Renter may seek mediation (see back page) before filing Small Claims or other Civil action. The prevailing Party may recover her/his reasonable costs and attorney's fees incurred in a legal action to enforce or interpret the provisions of this agreement or to recover possession of the rental property.

9. INVENTORY CHECKLIST

The inserted Inventory Checklist is provided to avoid arguments over the condition of the rental. It is designed to equally protect the Owner and the Renter from being held responsible for damages they did not cause, and to minimize disputes over the return of deposits. (See Check list for instructions.)

The Owner specifically agrees to complete the following repairs or improvements by the following dates:
Repair or Improvement   date

_____

_____

_____

_____

_____

_____

_____

_____

_____

ADDITIONAL AGREEMENTS

_____

_____

_____

_____

_____

_____

_____

_____

_____

_____

CAUTION: THIS IS A LEGALLY BINDING AGREEMENT; MAKE SURE YOU UNDERSTAND ALL OF ITS PROVISIONS.

The signing of this agreement acknowledges the Owner's receipt of $_____from the Renter for_____

_____

This Agreement is entered into this_____day of_____ 19____.

_____

Owner's signature   Renter's signature

_____

Owner's Agent   Renter

Both the Owner and the Renter shall receive a copy of this Agreement.

ANY CHANGES IN RENT OR OTHER CONDITIONS OF THIS AGREEMENT MUST BE AGREED TO IN WRITING BY BOTH PARTIES.

INVENTORY CHECKLIST

Both the Owner and the Renter should fill out this Checklist within three days after the Renter moves in, and again when the Renter moves out. Both the Owner and the Renter should sign and receive a copy of the Checklist after each Inspection.

In completing the inventory checklist, BE SPECIFIC and check carefully. Among the things to look for are dust, dirt, grease, stains, damages, and wear. Cross out items which do not apply, and add additional items as needed.

ITEM	QUANTITY (If applicable)	CONDITION ON ARRIVAL	ON DEPARTURE Note deterioration beyond reasonable use and wear for which tenant is alleged to be responsible.
LIVING ROOM			
Floor Covering			
Walls & Ceiling			
Tables & Chairs			
Sofa			
Windows (draperies, screens, etc.)			
Doors, including hardware			
Light Fixtures			
BEDROOMS			
Floor Covering			
Walls & Ceiling			
Closet, including doors & tracks			
Desk(s) & Chairs			
Dresser(s)			
Bed(s), frame, mattress - check both sides for stains - pads, bx sprng)			
Windows (draperies, screens, etc.)			

ITEM	QTY.	CONDITION ON ARRIVAL	CONDITION ON DEPART.
BEDROOMS (Continued)			
Doors, including hardware			
Light Fixtures			
BATHROOMS			
Floor Covering			
Walls & Ceiling			
Shower & Tub (walls, door, tracks)			
Toilet			
Plumbing Fixtures			
Windows (draperies, screens, etc.)			
Doors, including hardware			
Light Fixtures			
KITCHEN			
Cupboards			
Floor Covering			
Walls & Ceiling			
Counter Surfaces			
Stove & Oven, Range Hood, (broiler pans, grills, etc.)			
Refrigerator (ice trays, butter dish, etc.)			
Sink and Garbage Disposal			
Tables & Chairs			

ITEM	QTY.	CONDITION ON ARRIVIAL	CONDITION ON DEPART.
KITCHEN (continued)			
Windows (draperies, screens, etc.)			
Doors, including hardware			
Light Fixtures			
HALLWAYS OR OTHER AREAS			
Floor Covering			
Walls & Ceiling			
Closets, including doors & tracks			
Light Fixtures			
Air Conditioner(s)			
Filter			
Patio, Deck, Yard (planted areas, ground covering, fencing, etc.)			
Other (please specify)			

BEGINNING INVENTORY DATE _____, 19____

_____   _____

Owner's signature   Renter's signature

MOVING OUT INVENTORY DATE_____, 19____

_____   _____

Owner's signature   Renter's signature

DISCRIMINATION IN HOUSING

The Rumford Fair Housing Act makes it unlawful for an owner of housing that has received any kind of public assistance to refuse to sell, rent, lease or otherwise deny or withhold to any person or group of persons such housing accommodations because of race, color, religion, national origin, ancestry, sex, or marital status. If you think you have been discriminated against, call your local Fair Housing Commission_____
Housing & Urban Development (HUD)_____
_____
_____
_____

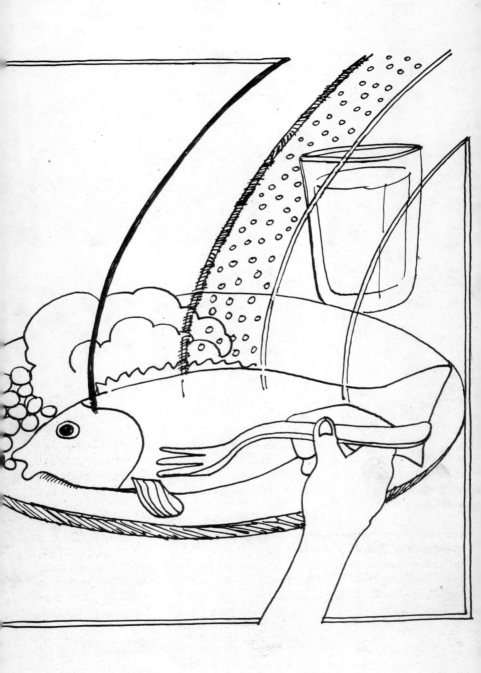

FOOD

Whether you eat in a college dining hall, a coop, an apartment shared with others or in your own place you will want to be eating right so that your mind and body are able to work at a high level. In order to assure a good diet you need to know about the Basic 4 Food Groups which are included in this section.

If you are in a living situation where you do all or part of the cooking you will want information on how to buy and prepare food so that it is inexpensive, delicious and healthful. You will also want some ideas in the tedious (sometimes) job of meal planning. We have included tips to make your shopping trips easier and more economical. There is also a section on tools to use in the kitchen so that you—and perhaps your guests—can cook and eat in style.

At the end of this section you will find empty pages for your favorite family recipes. A good bowl of soup really takes the chill off and goes a long way to easing feelings of loneliness. You might be surprised at just how easy it is to fix the wonderful soup you had at home, or perhaps at your grand-parents', and the smell while it's simmering is simply wonderful.

EATING FOR HEALTH . . . AND ENJOYING IT TOO!

Your body will work well for you providing you take the time and effort to feed it what it needs to function well. Good nutrition comes from knowing which foods are needed in order to promote good health. Many people think it's not worth the effort "cooking just for myself." They nibble on junk food, pick at whatever may be in the cupboard and spend much more money on eating out than they would if they bought food wisely and cooked at home.

In recent years there has been an information explosion about nutri-tion—and some confusion too. It's clear that the final word is not yet in. However, it is generally agreed that in order to eat nutritionally sound meals you will need to know about the Basic 4 Food Groups. If you eat the right number of servings from each of these groups daily you will be assured of getting the proper balance of nutrients.

1. Milk Group: This group is especially important for calcium and phosphorus; it also provides protein, riboflavin and other nu-trients. Adults need 2 or more cups daily.

2. Meat Group: This group provides important sources of protein, iron, B vitamins, and other nutrients. Non-meat eaters may substi-tute cheese, dry beans, eggs, peanut butter. Adults need 2 or more servings, 2-3 ounces each, daily.

3. Vegetable-Fruit Group: This group provides good sources of most vitamins and minerals. Adults need 4 or more servings, ½ cup each, daily.

4. Bread-Cereal Group: These foods offer B vitamins, some protein, and other nutrients. Bread and cereal products should be whole grain or enriched. Adults need 4 or more servings, 1 slice bread, 1 ounce dry cereal, ½ cup rice or pasta, daily.

Also needed are 4 to 8 cups of fluid per day.

The U.S. Senate Select Committee on Nutrition and Human Needs set forth the following suggestions for selecting and preparing food to meet the recommended dietary goals.

1. Increase consumption of fruits and vegetables and whole grains.

2. Decrease consumption of refined and other processed sugars and foods high in sugars.

3. Decrease consumption of foods high in total fat, and partially replace saturated fats, whether obtained from animal or vegetable sources, with poly-unsaturated fats.

4. Decrease consumption of animal fat, and choose meats, poultry and fish which will reduce saturated fat intake.

5. Except for young children, substitute low-fat and non-fat milk for whole milk, and low-fat dairy products for high fat dairy products.

6. Decrease consumption of butter fat, eggs and red meats.

7. Decrease consumption of salt and foods high in salt content.

Dieting

There seems to be no easy way to lose excess pounds despite the endless stream of wonder diets published in magazines and books and touted by T.V and movie stars.

It's not unusual for young people first away from home to either lose or gain a great deal of weight as their diet, their schedule and their eating habits are often vastly changed. We suggest you buy a calorie counter book and get a sense of the caloric value of different foods. A calorie is a measurement of energy. The food we eat contains calories which are either burned up as energy or stored as fat.

If you were to eat one extra tablespoon of butter (100 calories) each day for one year you would gain a little over 10 pounds in that year! 3500 calories will create one pound of body fat. In order to lose one pound of body weight, it is necessary to reduce your food intake by 3500 calories. So, if you have a weight-loss goal of 2 pounds a week, you will have to lower your daily calorie intake by 1000 calories per day.

When trying to cut calories the first thing to do is to cut out the high calorie foods that are low in nutritional value. Such foods include candy, potato chips, most sweet or salty munchies, and soft drinks. Substitute low-fat yogurt for mayonnaise or sour cream; use commercial "diet" margarine; sauté vegetables in broth rather than fat; select foods like chicken, fish and turkey which are naturally low in fat; use a non-stick pan for frying; use skim milk for cooking and drinking whenever possible.

Working with the information you now have about your nutritional needs from the 4 Basic Food Groups and the calorie counter, you can map out a sensible diet for yourself. If you find that you are still unable to lose weight you probably should consult with a nutritionist (often found in medical clinics) or with a doctor who specializes in weight-management problems.

Vegetarians

In the past decade many people have become vegetarians, i.e. non-meat eaters. Some vegetarians do not eat eggs; some eliminate dairy products; some allow fish and chicken in their diets. Before embarking on a vegetarian diet we suggest you read Frances Lappe's **Diet for a Small Planet,** for sound nutritional advice and delicious recipes.

Frances Lappe points out that possibilities for a good vegetarian diet are almost endless. There are about 40 to 50 different commonly grown and eaten vegetables, 24 kinds of peas, beans and lentils, 20 fruits, 12 kinds of nuts, and 9 commonly eaten grains.

One of the first things to learn when following a vegetarian diet is how to combine plant foods so that the protein needs of the body can be met. Combinations of plants eaten together which are equal to animal proteins are peanut butter and bread, dried beans and corn, beans and rice, soybeans and sesame seeds, and milk products and grain.

All proteins are made of amino acids. Plant proteins are generally lacking or low in one or more of the eight essential amino acids which the body cannot make. In addition, the eight essential amino acids must be eaten in proper amounts in a meal so that all body proteins can be made. Any amino acids not eaten in the right amounts to go along with others eaten at the same meal are passed out of the body and the carbon part of the protein is stored in the body fat deposits.

You can see that it takes some new learning to be a healthy vegetarian if you were brought up eating meats, but there are innumerable books available and once you learn some basics you can proceed in good order.

STOCKING THE KITCHEN

To begin cooking even the most simple foods you will need non-perishable staples, such as salt, oil, flour, etc. Your first shopping trip will be a big and somewhat expensive one, but once you've stocked up on staples you won't find·yourself in the middle of a recipe without one of the basic ingredients.
Before your first big shopping trip, take the time to walk through several markets to develop a sense of the prices, the helpfulness of the personnel, the cleanliness of the store, and the feel of the place in general. You may decide to shop for canned goods and staples in one store and go to another for meats and produce. Health or natural food stores are "sprouting" in certain parts of the country. These stores will vary in quality and honesty as much as the large supermarket chains. Small neighborhood stores are wonderful when you run out of milk late at night but they are too expensive for everyday shopping.
Below are a number of hints to help you develop supermarket savvy:

1. Read the food section of the local newspaper—usually Wednesday evening or Thursday morning—to locate which stores have what on special for the coming week.

2. Store brands are less expensive than name brands and are often of equal quality.

3. Read labels! Manufacturers are required to list ingredients according to the amount contained in the product.

4. Labels also frequently give information on the number of servings and calories per serving contained in the package.

5. Right on the shelf itself you can find the unit price, i.e. how much you are paying per ounce or per foot for a brand. You can then cross-check other brands to see which is the best buy.

6. Products on the dairy shelf have "pull dates." These indicate when the item should be either sold or removed from the shelf. Keep in mind when you are going to use the product. Usually the freshest products are placed to the rear of the refrigerator or shelf.

7. Convenience foods are very expensive compared with the same item made at home. Check this out by looking at the cost of prepared rice mixes and then figuring what it would cost if you used bulk rice and added your own chicken bouillon flavoring and diced vegetables. A rule of thumb is that frozen dinners cost two to three times as much as making a meal from scratch. (And they are loaded with salt, which is not always a good idea).

8. Condensed and dehydrated soups are better buys than pre-watered soups.

9. Seasonal produce is always fresher and less expensive than produce which is out of season and must be shipped.

10. Processed meats (bologna, hot dogs, bacon) are expensive sources of protein, are high in salt and may contain nitrates which are suspected of being cancer-causing agents.

11. Pre-wrapped and individually sliced cheese is expensive compared to cheeses bought in bulk and kept bagged in the refrigerator.

12. Powdered milk is a great buy for cooking and drinking. The milk tastes best if it is made ahead and chilled. Some people compromise by using equal parts of powdered and whole milk.

13. Clip coupons to take advantage of the discounts! But remember, it's no bargain if you don't use it.

Staples you will want to stock in your kitchen include:

Flour: bleached, unbleached, whole wheat, and pre-sifted

Pastas: rice, noodles of every variety, spaghetti, barley, buckwheat groats (kasha). Look for pastas made with whole wheat or vegetable flour.

Dried beans: kidney, lima, lentil, garbanzo, black-eyed peas, soy. Dried beans are rich in protein, low in cost and highly nutritious. Beans with a little meat and/or vegetables can form the base for a wonderful, low-cost, high-flavor meal.

Eggs: brown or white (They have the same nutritional value.)

Grated cheese: adds protein and flavor to pasta dishes.

Canned/dried soups: use as whole meals, as gravy or as flavoring for beans and pasta.

Condiments: ketchup, steak sauce, mustard, lemon juice concentrate.

Sugar: white, brown and confectioner's.

Honey: a more nutritious sweetener than sugar.

Dried fruit: raisins, prunes, apricots, peaches, pears.

Seasonings: garlic powder, salt, pepper, tarragon, oregano, rosemary, basil, cinnamon, vanilla extract, etc. Buy herbs and spices in small quantities and keep away from heat as they lose their flavors.

Beverages: coffee - ground, decaffeinated, instant tea - black or herb, canned fruit or vegetable juices

Bread: Grocery stores have a wide variety of breads. Look in the phone book for the address of the "day-old" bread store which offers good bread at a savings. Bread will keep longer if refrigerated or frozen.

Crackers: Once opened, keep in a tin or refrigerate to keep fresh.

Cereals: hot cereals to be prepared and cold cereals. Now is the time to read labels! Avoid cereals with lots of sugar and empty calories.

Canned goods: tuna fish, tomato paste, garbanzo and kidney beans, chili peppers.

Paper goods: toilet paper, paper towels, plastic wrap, waxed paper, aluminum foil, napkins, lunch bags. These items are expensive but necessary. Try different brands and don't be taken in by fancy advertising. Often the "house" brands are the same quality as the more popularly known names. Stock up when prices get low.

STORING PERISHABLE FOOD

Perishable foods need to be used as soon after purchase as possible or stored at the right temperature and humidity to avoid loss of quality and/or spoilage.

The refrigerator:

1. Keep whole-grain flour in the refrigerator.

2. Keep vegetable oil in the refrigerator.

3. Green leafy vegetables keep their crispness and nutrition best in cold, moist air. Refrigerate vegetables in plastic and only wash just before using. Mushrooms are an exception: Pack in a brown bag to avoid moisture.

4. If you have the room, keep potatoes and onions in your refrigerator.

5. Keep bread, muffins and other grain products in the refrigerator.

6. Any refrigerated food that loses quality through drying should be covered with foil or put in an air-tight container.

7. An open box of baking soda in the mid-to-rear section of the refrigerator will absorb unpleasant or strong food odors.

The freezer:

The freezer space in a refrigerator does not give a temperature of 0 degrees—the temperature needed for prolonged freezing. However, your freezer compartment can be used effectively.

1. Freeze bread and take pieces out as needed.

2. Wrap hamburger patties, chops, steaks, and breakfast sausages individually. If you do not use them as planned (the evening of the day defrosted) the chops and steaks can be used the following day provided you keep them refrigerated. Once defrosted, hamburger and sausage should be used immediately or thrown out.

3. Do not thaw and then re-freeze items, especially meat, fish and poultry.

4. Buy frozen vegetables in the large, economical "poly" bags and use only the amount needed. Close the bag with a rubber band.

5. Make enough soup or stew for two or three meals, and freeze the extra. Eat within three weeks time.

Spoiled Foods

Indications of spoilage that make food unpalatable but not hazardous to your health are a rancid odor and the flavor of fats caused by oxidation. This may take the form of slime on the surface of meat, fermentation of fruit juices due to yeast growth and mold on bread and cheese. The spoiled parts of these foods can be removed and the food can be eaten without risk of illness. However, the nutritional value of spoiled, old or poorly-wrapped foods is low and the taste does suffer.

Food Poisoning

A foul odor and a sour taste in bland foods are indications that there has been bacterial spoilage which is dangerous. Even more lethal are those foods which look and taste good but are contaminated and will cause food poisoning if eaten.

Most bacteria thrive best under the same conditions we enjoy. They need warmth, moisture, and food to survive and reproduce. Bacteria prefer food which is high in protein and moisture. Some of the worst culprits are potato salad, chicken, chicken soup, barbequed pork, lemon tarts and custards.

There are several bacteria which, given the proper growing conditions, infect the host food. The illness that results may be one of any number including salmonellosis, staphylococcal poisoning, botulism, trichinosis, or bacillus cereus poisoning.

Most food poisoning is a result of improper food handling or storage. Food that has been prepared by persons carrying a bacterial infection or prepared in a place which is not kept sanitary are favorite breeding grounds. Food that is not thoroughly cooked or that is left to sit out at room temperature are also good candidates for breeding bacteria.

Beware of foods that have been left to sit on a buffet—neither on ice nor on a heating tray. Be especially cautious about eating foods made with milk or eggs, like potato salad, that have been sitting in the sun as happens on many picnics.

Food poisoning hits within hours of ingesting the food. Symptoms include abdominal pain, diarrhea, chills, fever, nausea. Some foodborne illnesses last only a few hours and others take several days to leave the system. It is best to consult a doctor if the symptoms do not lessen within a few hours.

FOOD STAMPS

The federal government sponsors the Food Stamp Program to meet the nutritional needs of low-income people. Food stamps are coupons in different dollar amounts which can be used like money to buy food at stores which accept the coupons.

Food stamps may not be used for nonfood items such as tobacco, liquor, dog food, vitamins, or soap. Food stamps cannot be exchanged for money.

You may be considered as a food stamp household alone, with your family, or with a group of persons who buy, store and cook their food together and share expenses. To determine if you are eligible for food stamps call or go to your local county welfare office where you will fill out an application.

If you need food immediately be sure to make that need known to the eligibility worker. Any application for food stamps must be answered within 30 days of application.

KITCHEN TOOLS

Whipping up a delicious dinner can be done with only one pot and one wooden spoon. However, to add variety to your menu and interest to the task of cooking, a few additional utensils are necessary and helpful.

Cookware

Cookware—pots and pans—are the most basic tools in any kitchen. As you look around in a kitchenware department, you'll see that cookware ranges from the very cheap to the very expensive and is made in a variety of materials, styles and colors. As you do more cooking, you'll develop your own preference for the kind of cookware—cast aluminum, cast iron, stainless steel, porcelain-coated steel—that you most enjoy using. When you're just starting out, it's a good idea to use different types of cookware before investing in a complete set. You'll find useable, low-cost, second hand cookware at stores like Goodwill, garage and church rummage sales. Shopping for bargains is fun too! Test to see if the item is sturdy, look for cracks and chips, and don't be taken in by pretty colors or by items that claim to do 1,000 and 1 jobs!

Since eating off tarnished silverware often tastes metallic, think about buying an inexpensive set of stainless steel knives, forks and spoons. Don't forget dishes to eat from—perhaps you can get some extras from home or look for good values in rummage shops.

Here is a list of some basic kitchen tools you will need:

☐ Large serving/mixing bowl   ☐ 10'' bread knife
☐ Medium serving/mixing bowl   ☐ 8'' slicer
☐ Collander   ☐ 5'' utility knife
☐ Large cooking pot (spaghetti cooker)   ☐ 4'' paring knife
☐ 2-quart pot with cover   ☐ Knife sharpener
☐ 12'' frying pan   ☐ Wooden spoons
☐ 7'' frying pan   ☐ Soup ladle
☐ Tea kettle   ☐ Spatula
☐ Measuring cups   ☐ Potato/carrot peeler
☐ Measuring spoons   ☐ Grater
☐ Cutting board   ☐ Large metal spoon
☐ Broiler pan   ☐ Eggbeater
☐ 9''x13'' baking pan

If possible, try to purchase any of the above items in their oven-proof form. Having bowls and pots that can go from the refrigerator to the oven and vice versa will make your equipment much more versatile.

For those of you who will be living in a dorm, a bit more ingenuity is required. Most dorms provide next to nothing in the way of kitchen facilities; check out what your college has. When planning on what to bring with you, analyze your eating and snacking habits and then plan ways of accommodating them. Usually, the bare essentials include:

1. A "hot pot" for boiling water quickly to make coffee, tea, instant soup, or hot chocolate mixes

2. Ceramic mugs or glasses

3. Spoons, forks and knives

4. A can-opener

MEAL PLANNING

In order to save time and money it's a good idea to plan meals a week in advance and then shop all at once. It may be that this seems too structured or too big a task and if so, we suggest you begin by planning meals three days at a time. You'll probably be going out for some meals so look at your calendar before going so you don't buy food that will spoil if not used.

Nothing is a bargain if you don't need it and won't use it! But you can find bargains, or at least good buys, if you learn to shop for in-store and seasonal specials. To do this you will want the local paper on that day of the week (usually it's Wednesday) that has the food ads. This issue of the paper also gives recipes using seasonal foods and can be a big help in planning meals.

Meal planning will also be considerably eased if you think of breakfast and lunch as fairly standard and keep on hand bread, cereal, eggs, peanut butter, cheese, cans of fish (tuna, sardines) and canned or dehydrated soups. These foods keep well, can be fixed in various ways and can be used for dinner should you be rushed. Sometimes people who live alone eat their big meal at noon, in a restaurant, and then have a lighter menu at dinner. If your budget allows you to do this it's a good plan and certainly simplifies meal planning and cooking.

We have come to think of certain foods as fitting certain meals but it can be interesting and nutritionally sound to shake this up. Soup is a hearty way to start off the day and with toast and butter it's a complete meal. Pancakes can be eaten for dinner as well as for breakfast. A serving of bacon or cottage cheese (protein) and fruit would make this a healthy meal. (You would want to have had some green vegetables and more protein during the earlier part of the day.)

When cooking for yourself it is not unusual for enthusiasm and imagination to fly out the window. You can settle for a ground beef patty, mashed potatoes, green salad, and oreo's for dessert. While this is an OK meal you would probably find it boring if you had it too often.

Menu planning usually starts with a meat, a starch, a vegetable, or maybe a salad. We are not going to include dessert as an integral part of menu planning. Perhaps it would be helpful for you to draw yourself a chart such as the following:

MEAT	STARCH	VEGETABLE	SALAD
Lamb patty (broiled)	Baked Potato	Baked, gingered carrots	lettuce or spinach
Baked chicken	Brown rice	Steamed zuccini	grapefruit/avocado
Grated parmesan cheese	Spinach noodles	Sliced tomatoes	Greens

If you feel confused about what to serve with what, take a little time to browse through some cookbooks and once in a while buy a "home magazine." Some of these magazines have monthly food planning menus from which you can get a sense of what goes with what, how to cook enough for several meals and how to use the same basic recipe in a variety of ways. Make sure you get your favorite recipes from your family members.

ENTERTAINING

Cooking for guests can be more fun than cooking only for one, but don't plan such complicated meals that by the time your guests arrive you are exhausted, resentful and just wish they'd all go home. To make entertaining enjoyable, make your menu simple, try it out on yourself and perhaps your best friend, and get a feel for what it entails. This will help you to know how to allow guests to assist with the dinner by bringing a dessert or some appetizers to have beforehand. Pot-luck parties are also fun as people get to bring one dish and then enjoy what others brought to round out the meal. Remember, a relaxed host and a comfortable atmosphere are more important than good food.

FAMILY RECIPES

When leaving home, take with you your favorite family recipes and the names of cookbooks that your relatives recommend. Although your favorite cookie recipe will probably be the first thing you ask for, try to get foods from all categories—soups, salad dressings, ethnic specialties—that will stand you in good stead. It is helpful to organize this information in some kind of index file or book.

_____

_____

_____

_____

_____

_____

_____

_____

_____

_____

_____

_____

_____

_____

_____

_____

_____

_____

CLOTHING

BUYING AND CARING FOR YOUR CLOTHING

What a person wears is a personal matter depending on life styles, taste, attitudes, climate, and money. We live in an era in which the norms of what is right to wear are quite wide, and stores provide us with options galore. All of this freedom to express ourselves through dress can, in fact, be confusing; but with some thought anyone can build a wardrobe which fits individual needs, personality and budget.

In this section, we discuss how to start building a wardrobe with accents of fun which won't ruin your budget. We also suggest that you don't buy too much before finding out about your new locale. Included are tips for making shopping trips pay off for you and some off-beat areas for finding good clothing bargains.

There is a section discussing the need to understand the various modern fabrics used in clothing so that you can give your clothes proper care. Space is provided so that your parents can fill in tips on laundering and laundry aids. Information on how to remove common stains is included.

Since your junior high school days, you've probably been selecting your own clothing with your parents paying all or part of the bill. At this point, if you're going on with your education, your parents may continue their support, or it may be expected that you will buy your own clothes using the income from your summer or school-year job. If you're headed for full-time employment it may be assumed that you'll be paying for all your own clothing. You might need an advance, to be paid back later, so that you can start work looking presentable. Whatever the arrangements, you will now want, more than ever before, to spend your clothing money wisely.

If you're leaving home, either for school or work, bring your old clothes that are in good condition. Wait until you see what the mode of dress is in your new place before making additions to your wardrobe. Although fashion magazines and stores may be pushing the "Return to the Classics" look or the "Femme Fatale" look, you may find everyone on campus still spends Saturday night in jeans and batik thermal underwear tops. In vocational training programs, there are frequently expectations or codes on how trainees should dress. You will feel quite angry, not to mention broke, if you've made major outlays only to discover that all trainees must wear something else. So wait. There are stores wherever you go.

Some people build a wardrobe for long-term use while others want a wardrobe for NOW, with a new one for next year. The first approach can result in a rather conservative look, while the second is outrageously expensive. We suggest a combination: Build a wardrobe around well-made, neutral-colored pants, skirts and jackets, and add shirts, blouses and accessories which are fashionable. By 'fashionable' we mean those styles, colors and materials which are in the stores this year. Next year there will be changes—that's how the clothing industry makes money. You won't lose money or the fun of being in style if you depend on your basics and then add fun pieces each year. Of course, you can wear last year's 'in' fashion for several seasons—in fact, until it wears out!

Tips for Buying

Some people love the enormous selection of merchandise available in large department stores and others feel so overwhelmed that they become too paralyzed to buy anything. Take some time to find which store or stores feel best to you, have the kind of clothing you like and offer the price range you can best afford. It's not always easy to be a smart shopper but it can be done if you take some effort and think about the following suggestions.

1. Decide whether you're shopping for something specific or just want to add something to your wardrobe. If the latter is the case, have in mind what you're going to be needing as the new season approaches and whether you have the money for fun additions. If you don't have the money, it may be wise not to venture into shopping situation where you will make impulse buys.

2. Don't go shopping on a "fat day." Nothing will look right and you'll have a miserable time.

3. Wear comfortable shoes. Finding clothing can mean lots of walking around.

4. Wear clothes that you can get in and out of easily.

5. Don't buy clothes without trying them on, even if you are sure of your size and have always worn the same brand.

6. When you look at a garment, evaluate what else it will go with in your wardrobe. Don't buy a shirt if you have nothing to wear it with unless you can also afford to buy new pants or a skirt.

7. Check the care instructions which are now sewn into most clothes. Learn the basics of fabric care and don't buy garments requiring care that you are unable or unwilling to give, e.g. silk and wool need to be dry cleaned.

8. Don't buy something just because you don't want your shopping trip to have been "a waste of time."

9. Don't automatically turn away from sales racks—you may find some very good buys on basics. On the other hand, just because something is on sale—even at 75 percent off—it's no bargain if you don't need it, don't have anything to wear it with, or don't have anywhere to wear it to!

10. Shop sales. One of the benefits of having a charge account from a store is that you will receive notice of Sale Days before the sale is

advertised to the public. Seasonal sales or end-of-month sale days can be budget stretching if you do your thinking about what your wardrobe needs **before** going to the sale.

11. Wise shopping does not always equal cheap shopping. Although price is an important consideration, there are some items which are worth a higher dollar if it ensures a higher quality. A 100% wool sweater will last years longer than a cheaper acrylic one. Evaluate the purpose and lifetime of the garment you are purchasing. Some of the more common long-term buys traditionally include sweaters, coats, leather shoes or boots, and jewelry.

Re-Run Shops

Nearly-new, re-run or second-hand shops have always existed in large cities but now they are in towns all across the country. These stores operate by taking used clothing—in good condition—and reselling it, usually with the store owner and garment owner sharing in the profit. In such stores, the customer pays far less than in shops with new merchandise. Not only are the stores good for buying clothing, they are also good if you want to sell used clothes. The "mistake" that looks awful on you might be sold at a nearly-new shop. While you won't recoup anywhere near the purchase price, you might get a few dollars and at least you won't have to face the "mistake" whenever you open your closet.

Get to know the character of the different re-run shops in your town. Learn what kind of clothes each of them specializes in. In larger cities, you can often find re-run shops which carry evening clothes for a fraction of the original cost. For that special dance or party, you might do well to check out what's available in the re-run shops before making a costly purchase for a garment for which you'll have little future use.

Rummage Sales and Benefit Shops

If you learn the "art" of rummage shopping, you can find handsome bargains at rummage sales and benefit shops. The "art" of finding good sales lies in having a sociological eye, or nose, or both. That is, you have to find out which churches, hospitals and agencies have auxiliaries made up of the well-to-do in the community. The auxiliary (usually women who give their time and/or services to a cause) donate items from their own wardrobes which they no longer wear, and are often able to persuade local merchants to donate goods which have not sold. If it bothers you to seek out bargains this way, remember that your money is going toward worthwhile community causes.

Read the Label

In 1973, a clothing-care labeling law was passed specifying that most garments and yardgoods have a sewn-in label instructing how the garment should be cleaned. Most labels also include information on the fiber content of the garment. It will save you time, money and energy to know whether certain fibers can go into a washing machine, a dryer or need ironing.

Nowadays, very few items are composed 100 percent of any single fiber. This is because every fiber, natural and man-made, has inherent pluses and minuses. For example, cotton is a wonderful-feeling material: It is strong; it takes color well; it is resistant to perspiration, and it is cool to wear. But cotton is not wrinkle resistant. A 100 percent cotton shirt will need to be ironed every time it's washed and will wrinkle from just ordinary wear. If the cotton is blended with polyester, a man-made fabric, the garment will not wrinkle and needs no ironing after laundering. Polyester, used alone, is not an absorbent fiber and is susceptible to oily stains. Thus, by blending cotton with polyester we have a superior fabric which is both strong and easy to care for.

Wool, another natural fiber, is colorfast and can't be beat for warmth. But wool needs special care in cleaning. Mix wool and polyester, and you still have a garment with all the virtues of wool but which won't shrink and doesn't need blocking after being washed.

Different synthetic materials are sold under various trade names such as Antron, Dacron, Kodel, Avril, Acrilan, Orlon, etc. Before you buy a garment read the care label, ask the salesperson what she knows about the advantages or disadvantages of the material and be sure you are clear on the cleaning instructions. If you stain a garment and you're not sure how to treat the stain, it is probably least expensive in the long run if you take the garment to a reputable dry cleaner.

FAMILY LAUNDRY HINTS

Always read the manufacturer's label on how to care for the fabric.

How to sort clothing for washing:

For automatic washers, use the following detergent:_____
_____
_____

Use bleach on the following fabrics:_____
_____
_____

For hand washing of delicate fabrics, use:_____
_____
_____

For hand washing of woolens, use:_____
_____
_____

Use a dry cleaner for:_____
_____
_____

Other information on laundry:_____
_____
_____

Stains are difficult to get out the longer they stay in the material. Once set, stains may be difficult to remove. It's important to know what the stain is and the fiber content of the material (usually found on the label). If you're not sure whether the color or fabric will be affected, test on an inconspicuous area like a hem. Always launder washable fabrics immediately after treating a stain.

Products you may need

Brand
Names

Prewash soil & stain remover_____
Enzyme Presoaks_____
Chlorine bleaches_____
Detergents_____
Bar soap_____

REMOVING COMMON STAINS

Blood: Soak in enzyme presoak product in cool water. Then launder as usual.

Chewing gum: Harden the stain with an ice cube & rub until gum crumbles off.

Chocolate: Scrape off as much of stain as possible, using a dull knife. Wash the fabric in warm soapy water. Sponge stubborn stains on white fabrics with hydrogen peroxide and rinse thoroughly.

Fruit juices: Use an enzyme presoak product. Launder as usual. If the stain remains, use bleach on it. *Important*— If a fruit stain has been ironed, it will probably not come out.

Grease stains: (bicycle & car grease, butter, cooking oils, margarine, mayonnaise) Pretreat with a heavy-duty liquid laundry detergent or prewash soil & stain remover. For heavy stains, place stain face down on paper towels and apply dry-cleaning solvent to back of stain. Let dry, then run in liquid detergent. Rinse and launder.

Milk & Ice Cream: Soak in warm water with an enzyme presoak product. Wash as usual.

Mustard: Apply a prewash soil & stain remover. Rinse and launder using chlorine bleach if safe for fabric. Should color of fabric change, use ammonia for fresh stains and vinegar for old. Rinse and launder in hottest water safe for color & fabric.

Grass: Sponge the stain with alcohol and then wash in hot water and bar soap rubbing the fabric well. If stain persists, use bleach as directed.

Wine & soft drinks: Soak in an enzyme presoak or oxygen bleach using hottest water safe for fabric. Launder. If stain remains, launder again, using chlorine bleach if safe for the fabric.

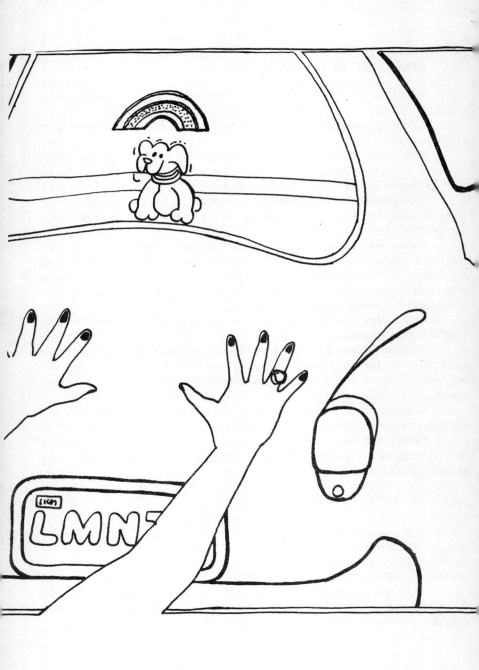

BUYING A CAR

"When Four Wheels May Be Too Many"

If you think you want or need a car when you leave home, read this section carefully. The cost of owning a car, its upkeep, and insurance can be a heavy strain on your monthly budget.

In this section there is a questionnaire designed to help you ask why you need a car and what features you need in a car. Along with suggestions on what to look for when test driving cars, there is also a checklist so that you can keep track of the important information you gather.

How to shop for a car loan is touched upon here, but you will find more detailed information on how to get a loan in the chapter on Money Matters. Automobile insurance is also discussed.

SHOPPING FOR A CAR

Owning a car is a big expense. Monthly payments, upkeep and insurance can use up a large portion of your monthly budget. So, before assuming you'll need a car, check out the transportation system where you'll be living. Some colleges only allow upperclassmen to have cars on campus, and a large number of communities are becoming so ecology-minded that buses and bikes are the preferred mode of transportation.

Eventually (statistically) you will own a car! It is likely that your first car will be a used one, and it's most important that you know the difference between used and abused. It takes skill to know what to look for in a used car, but it can be done.

Whether you're looking at cars on a lot or through a private party, here are some things to remember:

1. Sedans are sturdier than convertibles. The body frame is stronger and deteriorates less rapidly.

2. Many unnecessary options tend to age quickly and drain power from a car (such as air conditioning, etc.)

3. If you are buying from a dealer, you will only get a limited guarantee, good for a month or two. Find out and get it down in writing exactly what the guarantee covers. Buying from a private party means no guarantee at all.

4. You can also find used cars for sale at auctions (City, State and County), car rental agencies, taxi companies, and others who operate fleets of cars and usually sell their cars after they've been in use for a few years. Newspapers carry notices of such auctions when they're open to the public. Usually these cars have been well maintained and may be a good buy.

5. Oftentimes the price being quoted is only a starting point. You can bargain with both private parties, used car dealers and new car agencies. Comparison shop!

Danger Signs

1. Signs of repeated or severe accidents (mismatched paint or metal

stripping). A severely beat up car may have suffered engine and body damage that no mechanic can repair.

2. Extensive rusting on the lower portion of the body.

3. Oil under the hood may be a sign of a severe oil leak.

4. Headlights and radio that don't work may be caused by a faulty electrical system which is expensive to repair.

The "Lemon Peeler" test

After you've driven and given a used car the best inspection you can, bring it in for an inspection to a reliable mechanic. The mechanic should give the car a check-up which would include cylinder compression, front-end alignment, brake linings, frame, and cooling and exhaust systems. You should expect to pay anywhere up to $50 for such an inspection, and you can consider it money well spent if it saves you from investing in a "lemon" of a car!

Shopping for a loan

The costs and other conditions of borrowing can differ significantly from lender to lender. Try to talk with at least four lenders to get a good idea of what's available. The jargon of banks and lending institutions may seem beyond comprehension, but don't be afraid to ask questions - they are in business to make loans and they're not doing you a favor.

Insurance

Insurance against liability claims, physical damage and other driving perils is a virtual necessity not only to protect yourself, but to fulfill "financial responsibility law" for drivers in certain states. The law states that you must be able to prove that you can pay for any damages you cause to people and property with your car.

A way to keep the cost of insurance down, especially if the car is old and has a fairly low value, is to consider not getting physical damage or comprehensive insurance at all if the cost of the coverage is out of proportion to the car's value.

When shopping for insurance, check with several companies since rates can vary significantly even for identical coverage. Some insurance companies give discounts if, for example, you haven't had a ticket or been in an accident, don't smoke, are a good student, etc. Check around and again, don't be put off by the jargon but go ahead and ask questions so that you can make an intelligent decision that best fits your needs and your budget.

WHAT I NEED IN A CAR

1. Transportation
     a. *less than 20 miles a day* _____
     b. *Heavy duty freeway travel*
        over 50 miles a day _____
     c. *Weekend dating and Leisure* _____

2. Impress others _____

3. Carry building materials _____

4. Carry skis _____

5. Haul boat/trailer _____

6. Share a ride with 3 others
    for everyday commuting _____

7. Cross-country trips once or twice
    a year to visit parents & family _____

8. Transport goods _____

9. Carry young children _____

10. Just to go to the market
     once a week _____

11. One that gets more than 20
     miles to the gallon _____

12. Small enough to fit into
     carport _____

13. Head room/leg room for myself _____

14. Easy to repair _____

CARS THAT MEET MY SPECIFICATIONS

1. _____

_____

_____

2. _____

_____

_____

3. _____

_____

_____

4. _____

_____

_____

5. _____

_____

_____

6. _____

_____

_____

7. _____

_____

_____

8. _____

_____

_____

SHOPPING FOR A CAR
(Checklist)

Make of Car & Year	Dealer's Address	Name of Salesman/Mgr./ Private Party	Dealer's Phone No.	Pros	Cons	Sticker price vs. Price Offered You	Highest Price able to Pay

CHOOSING A PROFESSIONAL

HOW TO CHOOSE A PROFESSIONAL

Unfortunately, there is no easy way to find out which doctor, dentist, lawyer, accountant, or psychologist is the best one to represent or treat you. If you want to buy a typewriter, sewing machine, automobile tires, aspirin, tennis balls, or thousand of other items you can check to see what Consumer's Report says about what to look for and which products perform well on CR's tests. Be prepared to search and don't feel you have to hire the first person you find.

When most people need a professional they first ask friends for recommendations. This is an O.K. start, but it is even better to ask friends who work in a field related to your need (a court reporter or court stenographer knows more about lawyers than your average next door neighbor). Think about your friends and acquaintances and recall if any of them have recently had need for a specialist and be sure to ask them for their thoughts and recommendations. You can call the School of Dentistry or the School of Law, etc. at major universities and they will give the names of graduates practicing in your area. The Chief of Staff of your local hospital may help you define which sub-speciality you need and perhaps recommend a local physician. Law firms, the American Civil Liberties Union and the area Bar Association are helpful in referring caller to individual attorneys who can best handle your kind of case.

Most often we don't choose an expert until we need one and then, of course, we're pressed for time, perhaps in pain, and grateful if someone will see us quickly. Ideally, when choosing someone to advise us on personal matters we should begin the selection process before the need occurs. However, even when we have the necessary time it is difficult to make intelligent judgements about a person's competence in fields of specialization where we have little expertise.

Often we base our judgement on the person's age, looks and style. These factors have a place in our consideration but should not override the following:

1. Competence—You will want to find out if your specialist has the training and experience in the areas which are most important to you and if s/he knows when to refer you elsewhere.

Example: If you have a family history of diabetes you want a doctor who has an interest in and knowledge of this disease so that a preventative medical program can be developed for you.

2. Ability to Communicate—You will want to know that your specialist listens carefully to your concerns and can respond to you with clear recommendations and with as little jargon as possible.

3. Style—You will want to feel comfortable with your specialists manner, attitudes, style and know relevant biases.

Example: You do not want to work with a counselor who is judgmental, or an attorney who talks down to you, or a doctor who has no patience (respect) for your choice to be a vegetarian.

4. Business Methods—You will want to know how you will be billed (for tasks completed or for time); whether charges are made for phone calls; how records are kept; who covers if the doctor/dentist is on vacation; are appointments usually on time; are you billed if you miss an appointment?

It seems obvious that you won't find out about these four items until you actually work with the expert. It's far better to set an appointment and see how the doctor or the dentist works with a relatively minor problem rather than waiting until a major need arises. Eventually you must make a choice (you will need a dentist for preventative care) even though your information is not as complete as you would like. Remember also that no one person is going to be perfect—and you probably won't be a perfect client/patient either!

Once you do pick an expert you cannot just drop your case, your teeth or your body at his office and leave it all to him. You must be clear why you have sought help, what the history and the facts are (including relevant details even though they are embarrassing), and what you think you want/need help with. You must be willing to listen to your expert as s/he addresses the problem and possibly identifies complexities which you were unaware of and design a course of action which you had not considered. Remember, the specialist you have chosen is there to advise you but the responsibility for most decisions—including whether you continue to work with this particular expert—remains with you. In some communities, it is standard practice for the first interview to be free. Find out what is standard in your area.

III. THE INNER WORLD

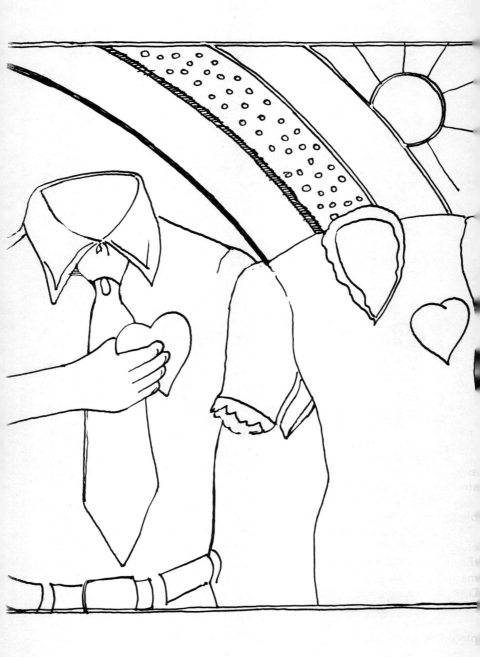

PERSONAL RELATIONS

"I Want to Hold Your Hand"

The one thing you take with you wherever you go is yourself. Moving away from what is familiar is a crash course in getting to know yourself, your strengths and your weaknesses.

In this Chapter we give some suggestions about how to feel comfortable living and being with people you didn't previously know.

Some people run from challenges and loneliness by finding someone else to cling to. In this section we discuss early marriage more as a warning than as an encouragement. A compatibility questionnaire for thinking about marriage is included along with a questionnaire on roommate compatibility. Discussion is included on how to improve relationships with roommates. Loneliness and its effects both positive and negative are looked into.

The question of how you are going to use your sexuality is also explored. We encourage you to develop your thinking about yourself as a sexual person who feels your values are as valid and good as anyone else's. We have included some resources for finding out more, on all aspects of interpersonal relations.

Learning about yourself can be an exciting adventure. You are bound to hit bumps, but these are great learning experiences if you take the time to look at what happened, put them in your memory bank, and then move on, using these experiences to draw upon later.

LEARNING NEW CUES

In your own family and community you know lots more about people and situations than you realized. We are all unaware, until our setting changes, of the many unwritten rules and unspoken expectations and values we have incorporated into our lives.

For example, when your father looked distantly into space and his eyes were misty, you knew he was worrying about his father in a rest home, and that now was not the time to intrude. You knew when your mother was laughing in a particular way and talking fast, it was because she was nervous about a business deal falling through, and that a hug would be welcome by her. You knew there was an 11 o'clock curfew in your home town, but no one paid attention to it, but you also knew that everyone was serious about the anti-litter law and it was strongly enforced by the police and citizens alike.

There will undoubtedly be new attitudes and expectations in the community you move to. The people, too, may communicate with words and cues you're not attuned to. You'd do best not to reach conclusions too quickly, i.e. make hasty assumptions. If your insides start yelling, "They're wrong," you know you're feeling scared and you need to back off and think things through. Take your time, use your eyes and ears to collect data and your mind to process it. Give yourself time to think and feel how, in fact, you really feel being here. The more receptive and sensitive you are to the differences, the richer you will find your new experience; the more open-minded you are, the more interesting friends you will make.

Sometimes you'll yearn for the security and comfort of knowing what to expect, but give yourself and others a chance. This is your first time out, and it takes time and patience to feel comfortable and to make sound judgments in any new situation.

ROOMMATES

When you first leave home, you will probably be living with at least one other person. In Hollywood-style fantasy, we imagine a roommate who is generous, kind, considerate, fun, and who becomes our dearest friend—always there for us, throughout our lives. Holding onto this fantasy will really get you into trouble! More realistically, a roommate can give you someone to talk to, cuts down on expenses, and may reduce the strain of adjusting to life away from your own home.

A successful living together situation takes cooperation from all concerned. Sometimes roommates don't make it; their life styles and rhythms don't fit at all, and it is best that a change be made. But never rush into such a change; see if you and the roommate you picked, were assigned to, or inherited along with the room, can find common ground to work things out. Here are some ideas that might be helpful:

1. **Your roommate is not a mind-reader and cannot possibly know what you are thinking, feeling, wanting. And you're not a mind reader either. Get into the habit of asking and telling each other whatever it is you want the other one to know.**

2. **If you're not clear about what your roommate is saying, ask, "Do you mean that_____?" until you're sure you understand. If you want to make sure that your roommate really heard what you meant to say, ask him or her, "Please tell me what you think I just said."**

3. **Honesty is the prime requisite for amiable coexistence. If either one of you feels annoyed or angry, or disappointed in something the other has or has not done, get it out into the open.**

4. **Be careful with the words you choose to express yourself. Being overly harsh or critical will put the other person on the defensive and will leave scars on the relationship you're trying to build. Try to express what is bothering you with "unloaded" words, and without accusations.**

5. **Being considerate helps a whole lot. This means thinking about how your actions are going to affect the other person. For example, when your roommate has a cold, it is inconsiderate for you to insist that the window near his/her bed be open so that you can get cross ventilation.**

6. **Be flexible. You think you can't go to sleep when there's a light on, but your roommate likes to read in bed. Try to think of a creative solution to cut the light from disturbing you and be willing to try sleeping with the light on. Of course, if this just doesn't work for you, then you and your roommate will have to solve the problem in another way.**

7. **It's fun, but not necessary, for you and your roommate to share interests, friends and activities. In fact, it's a good idea to be careful that you don't become such a close twosome that others feel unwelcome or hesitate about getting to know you.**

Make it a habit to sit down once a week, preferably at the same time and talk about how things are going. This is a time to ask questions, to straighten out misunderstandings, to make plans, and don't forget—it can also be a time for thanking a roommate for hearing what you requested last week and trying to do what you asked.

It's obvious as you look over these ideas that they also work in establishing strong relationships with friends as well as roommates. When you work things out with a roommate and have a successful living situation, you learn things about yourself as well as about other people. Most importantly, you learn that people do not "die" if there is disagreement and that conflicts can usually be resolved by honesty, a willingness to compromise and a sense of humor.

COMPATIBILITY QUESTIONNAIRE
FOR CHOOSING A ROOMMATE

You		Potential Roommate
_____	Food should be bought together	_____
_____	Meals should be eaten together	_____
_____	Chores should be divided equally	_____
_____	I am a day person	_____
_____	I like to talk in the morning	_____
_____	I like to play music loud	_____
_____	I am a vegetarian	_____
_____	I want to bring my girlfriend/ boyfriend home	_____
_____	Permission needed for guests to come to meals	_____
_____	Household expenses should be shared equally	_____
_____		_____
_____		_____

LONELINESS

Feelings of loneliness are certain to accompany the more pleasant feelings you will have on your first time out. In a new environment, whether you are shy or outgoing, you will need to become more assertive, to ask for what you want and to extend yourself to meet people. As the blues come on remind yourself that friendships rarely happen overnight. A rewarding friendship takes time, care, nurturing, and grows richer through shared experiences.

Start by getting to know the people in your dorm or your nearby work associates. This means being available as opposed to withdrawn. If your door's always closed and you never say "hi" and you take a book to the dining room it doesn't look like you're available (or much fun either). Being friendly, willing to lend a hand and generally open in your attitude gives others the idea that you are a nice and interesting person.

Classes are a natural place for meeting people because you have something in common to talk about. Often, right after class, everyone goes in his/her own direction. Don't hesitate to ask someone to coffee or lunch. You'll undoubtedly get some "no" responses but in the law of averages you'll come up with some takers too. And remember, saying no to a cup of coffee is not a rejection of you as a person! Some people find it easier to make an open invitation for anyone to join him or her for coffee rather than asking an individual. See what feels most comfortable for you and then try out some different approaches.

Joining clubs, organizations and religious groups is also a good place for finding people who share your interests. Don't expect the club here to be exactly like the one at home. Try to be open to the differences and see whether this is an activity you wish to remain in.

When your good friends or parents are not around to talk to, you are more tuned into yourself and more aware of the range of your emotions. This can be frightening and increase your feeling of loneliness. One way to alleviate these uncomfortable feelings is to keep a journal where you write down not only your activities but your moods and feelings. This helps to get your feelings outside of you. Over a period of time you can look back in your journal and you will probably see how low days are balanced out by higher ones, that feelings of confidence appear as well as unsureness and that both joy and sadness are there too.

Until you make some solid friendships you must act as your own best friend. You do this by tuning into yourself and finding out what you want, and what would make you feel better. You can give yourself some pleasures, like a concert, or a good breakfast out or a scenic bike ride. These are activities that are fun to share but you can do them on your own and enjoy your own company.

You can also pick up the telephone and make a splurge call to a friend who would understand. And you can give yourself a good cry. Find a comfortable place and let the tears come. You may be surprised at how relaxed you feel after letting yourself go.

Loneliness is a natural feeling. You've probably experienced it before; you're sure to experience it again. Now you have an opportunity to learn what helps you overcome this feeling.

RELIGIOUS CULT GROUPS

Within the past decade there has been an enormous growth of religious cult groups. These groups—there are an estimated 60 - 70 of them—are known under different names such as the Creative Community Project and Project Volunteer. Most popular around campus is the College Associate for the Research of Principles (CARP).

Recruitment into these groups is especially strong around university communities. During exam time or at the start of a new semester (when people often feel lonely, stressed, isolated, frightened) recruitment efforts, known as "love bombing," are greatly stepped up.

If you are approached by a cult recruiter the person will not identify him or herself as such. Rather, you will be invited to dinner, or to a week-end or week-long retreat, usually out of the city. You will be assured that you're being invited because, "You seem like such a good person." Most cult members are, in fact, well-educated persons who are dissatisfied with the materialism and inhumanity they see in today's world. The cults are appealing because they seem to offer a meaningful alternative. In reality, the cults are fronts for interest groups who use young persons to earn money and do servile tasks for the cult leaders.

Gary Scharff, an ex-moonie and former chief lecturer at the Unification Church, says that sometimes you don't find out where you are until you've suffered three weeks of emotional pummeling, sleep deprivation, poor diet, no privacy, and total undermining of your rational thinking process. Scharff warns to beware of strangers who invite you to a free meal. However, if you go to dinner and then are invited to a weekend retreat, make sure you talk with your parents or someone else you trust before going off because it becomes increasingly difficult to withdraw after you've been seduced in.

Throughout the history of the world people have joined groups out of a need to belong, to be valued and a wish to participate. Groups that are open about their goals and functioning, that allow members to leave at will, are very different from the cults we have been referring to above.

THOUGHTS OF EARLY MARRIAGE

It's not unusual for some young people to begin thinking of getting married as soon as—or even before—they leave home. They talk about feeling lonely, about wanting someone to take care of them and about how marriage would fill an emptiness they feel inside. Further discussion reveals that they are uncomfortable with their freedom. No longer under the control of their parents, they are confused and a little frightened by the many options open to them in regard to spending their time, energy and money. They are concerned about their ability to cope with the demands of the adult world.

Getting married can give the illusion of security. Many people use marriage as a way to avoid new challenges. However, marriage between young people (before either partner is twenty-one) has little chance of succeeding. Statistically, three out of five of these youthful marriages end within five years. Those marriages that do last report that the strain of marrying young was great and that their lives were severely limited by the decision to marry young. This is especially so if there was a pregnancy and thus the young couple was tied down immediately with the heavy responsibilities that having a family brings.

Ideally, there are certain "life tasks" which each person needs to complete between the time of leaving home and getting married. Some of these include:

—**knowing that you can care for yourself;**

—**knowing that you are financially self-sufficient;**

—**finding you are comfortable in varied situations and with a variety of people;**

—**being able to be emotionally open and to relate deeply with at least a few people outside of your own family.**

Once these tasks are accomplished—or at least well underway—there will be a solid sense of self worth which will enable you to proceed with seeking a mutually satisfying relationship. Of course it takes time, probably no less than a few years, to get to this point. The best marriages are made when two people come together each feeling good about themselves, their values and their ability to cope with the world, and each willing to make room for the other person.

There are no love relationships without problems, however, and the ways of dealing with them are as varied as the couples themselves. Before getting married, it's important to know where your trouble spots as a couple are likely to be. Ask yourself what it is that you **don't** like about the other person, and then honestly assess what that will mean to you and to your relationship. People who enter a marriage thinking that they will change their partner's behavior are most often very disappointed. It's highly unrealistic to think you'll find a perfect fit with anyone, but certain traits, characteristics, "dislikes" are more important than others. Take a look at the Marriage Compatibility Questionnaire to get an idea how compatible you and your potential mate may be.

Before getting married, you may find it helpful to talk with a counselor and sort out your hopes and expectations. Counseling resources are under Emotional Stress.

MARRIAGE COMPATIBILITY QUESTIONNAIRE

(discuss your opinion with your partner)

Partner A		Partner B
_____	At least one of us should be working when we get married.	_____
_____	I want to go back to school sometime during our marriage. (When?)	_____
_____	The person I marry should have friends other than me.	_____
_____	My partner should be able to accept constructive criticism.	_____
_____	The person I marry should be of the same religion as I.	_____
_____	I want children in my marriage. (When?)	_____

When I marry I plan to be sexually monogamous. (Have sex only with my mate.)

_____

I expect my partner to be monogamous.

I will move to a new city if my partner gets a better job than I have.

It is expected that both of us work during the marriage.

One person will be the "boss" in the marriage.

All decisions involving both of us will have to be agreed upon by both of us.

All of our money will go into one bank account.

The chores in the house will be shared equally.

If there are problems we cannot solve ourselves I want us to seek professional help.

Feel free to add to this questionnaire items that are important to you.

If you find you have several points of disagreement, you may want to reconsider your decision to marry. Another alternative is to seek relationship counseling.

LEGAL QUESTIONS REGARDING MARRIAGE

Marriage is a personal, a legal and sometimes a religious contract. Every state in the union has its own laws relating to marriage and to the dissolution of marriage. Below are some questions you will want to find out about marriage laws in the state you intend to marry in. Information can usually be obtained from the county office of the Registrar.

1. What is the age of marriage without parental consent?

2. Which, if any, premarital exams are needed? In many states, certificates providing freedom from diseases such as syphilis and German measles are required.

3. What is needed in order to obtain a marriage license?

4. Who may solemnize the marriage (judge, minister, etc.)?

5. Are you required to have premarital counseling?

6. Does the state you reside in recognize "common law" marriage, and what does recognition mean?

Marriage is much easier to get into than to get out of! You may want to know about the laws regarding dissolution of marriage in your state. Many young people decide they are going to live together rather than marry. This decision can often lead to tension and parental disapproval. Are you ready?

If you decide to live together you should know the legal ramifications. The book, **Cohabitation Handbook,** by Morgan D. King, an attorney, offers the following proposed rules:

1. Keep separate bank, credit and income tax accounts.

2. Advertise (i.e., let yourself be known) as single.

3. Use your own name.

4. Avoid pregnancy.

5. Before sharing in a financial or business venture, consult an attorney and have an agreement drawn up.

YOU AS A SEXUAL PERSON

Many older people believe that the young adults of today have few inhibitions or hang-ups about sex. The media portrays an "anything goes" attitude as rock music and movie stars appear displaying their sexuality in bold sounds and colors. It is our contention that many young people, too, have a difficult time accepting the "new sexuality" and often feel weird, or out of tune with the time.

All the while you have been living with your family and in your home town, you have been developing ideas and feelings about sex and about your own sexuality. If you are a male, the messages you have been given are different from those given a female. Many of you looked forward to being in a new environment where you would have the chance to experiment, to be free of the constraints put on you by your parents, and perhaps even by your friends. Once on your own, however, it is likely that you won't so easily shake off the early messages about sex.

It took time to develop your feelings about yourself as a sexual person. You may have very positive feelings about yourself as a sexual person, or you may have guilty and self-denying feelings. *Acting* sexually liberated is not the same as *being* comfortable with your sexual feelings. It is important to move into sexual experiences gradually, to give yourself time to explore and become familiar with your body and with your responses both physically and emotionally.

If you were lucky enough to grow up feeling comfortable with your body and your sexuality, it can still happen that moving to a new environment throws you off center. Also, just as you may be re-thinking other ideas you have long cherished, so too you may begin to re-examine your sexual code. Value decisions made at one age may need to be re-evaluated at another. Over your lifetime, you will have varying sexual needs.

It is essential for you to have accurate information on male and female anatomy, contraception, and venereal disease. There are innumerable books and magazines available from the bookshop, the library and the supermarket with such information. It is important when you read to be aware of the bias of the author. However, accurate information, important as it certainly is, does not address what is right or wrong for each person in building his or her sexual identity. Look around your campus or in your community (perhaps at the student health center, the Y, or at Planned Parenthood) for groups discussing relationships and sexuality. Make sure the atmosphere is open and non-judgmental, so that you can honestly explore your thoughts and feelings.

Our bias is that the most satisfying sexual experiences require the following elements: a relationship based on respect and equality; knowledge that you can enjoy sex without having intercourse; trust in yourself and your partner; honest communication; self-care in the form of contraception for yourself or your partner; a sense of humor; and time and privacy.

Homosexuality

Many young people go through the stage of being sexually attracted to people of their own gender. Some act out their sexual desires while others are merely aware of their attraction. Many people worry about these sexual feelings having been told that, "People like that are perverted." For many people this is just a stage in their sexual development that passes, or that is repressed—never again showing up in their lives. However, there is a small percèntage of people—estimated to be at least 10 percent of the population—who find that they prefer someone of their own gender.

There are many restrictions on people who are gay. Most states have laws forbidding same-sex practices. Most religions have strong words to say against homosexuality. With such strong social and religious feelings against homosexuality, a gay person can encounter many difficulties in living in a non-gay world. Being different from peers, s/he frequently has no one to talk with about his or her sexual preferences and awarenesses.

The whole topic of sexuality is so taboo in many communities that it is no wonder that young gay people feel completely cut off from getting information about their sexuality. In recent years, there have been some excellent books written on this subject. In some communities Gay Service Centers have been organized with counseling services for both the gay individual and his or her family. Some cities have gay hotlines, newspapers and groups that explore myths, realities and feelings. A growing number of politically active gay groups are working to change the laws which discriminate against gays.

Oftentimes, it is a problem for a straight person to discover that a good friend is gay. In most cases your friend is still your friend and will not want to have sex with you. Remember that a person is still the same person s/he was before you found out that s/he was gay.

If you find out that your roommate is gay, remember that gay people are just as choosy as straight people. Also, you can be quite clear with your roommate that having sex with him or her is not in your plans.

If you meet gays who do let you know that they want to know you sexually, just be assertive and clearly tell them that you aren't interested.

Remember: Homosexuality is not catchy. You will not "get it" by being friends with someone who is gay.

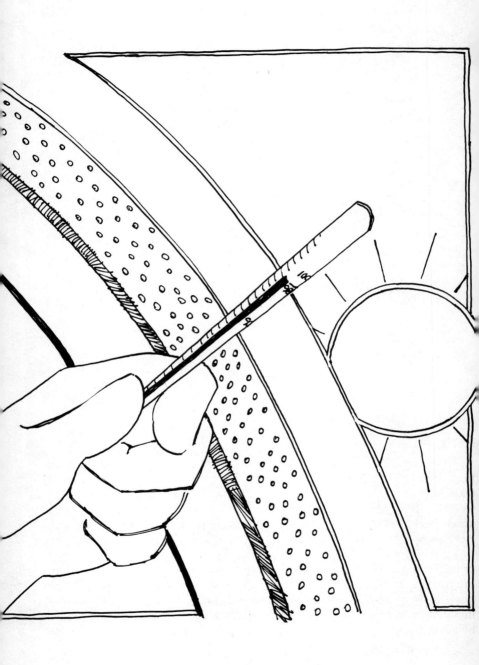

HEALTH

"... To good health and good friends and the time to enjoy them both." (Spanish New Year's toast.)

As a young child, your parent(s) supervised your health care. That is, from their learning and experience, they decided what you needed to do or take, including trips to a physician, dentist, clinic, etc., to remain physically well. Over the years, as you become more able and more knowledgeable about how your body functioned, the responsibility for health care shifted. Now, living away from home, it is your decision how to maintain good health.

In this section we discuss illness not only as an agent coming from out of the blue which we "catch," but as one of our bodies' direct responses to our physical and emotional environments. In the stress questionnaire developed by Dr. Thomas H. Holmes, we show that the stresses of daily life can take infinitely varied form, and that stress can pose just as much of a challenge to health as bacteria, viruses, poor nutrition, or chemicals. Also included in this section are two simple but very helpful procedures for calming yourself in a stressful situation.

We discuss when to see a doctor, how to choose a physician and how to prepare for a medical visit. We examine several methods of paying for medical care. We encourage you and your parents to complete the chart for home remedies for some of the more common medical problems.

People between the ages of 18-24 are faced with serious tasks including leaving home, preparing for a vocation, finding a secure sexual identity, and developing rich relationships outside of their original families. It is often helpful to seek help from a professional counselor/therapist in making these new moves and adaptations. We discuss how to go about choosing a counselor and the rights and responsibilities of both the client and the counselor.

All our lives we hear people wish us good health but until we experience a serious illness we are usually not appreciative of these particular thoughts. The health of most Americans, young and old, is damaged by the illness of "too much": too much fat in our diets; too much sitting; too much alcohol; too many drugs; and too much letting-the-doctor-fix-us. We hope that this section will help you to become more responsible in maintaining your health and knowing when and how to use professionals to augment your health needs.

HEALTH

Good health is not defined by the absence of disease but by the ability to function well within a given environment. Since the environment keeps changing, good health is a process of continuous adaptation to the many microbes, irritants, pressures, and stresses which are daily challenges.

We do not always catch a sore throat or get a yeast infection from out of the blue. Within our own systems and in the world, thousands of microbes of influenza, staphylococcus infections and many other diseases exist, and yet we do not usually succumb to illness. However, when we are feeling pressured in our work, have experienced an important loss or change in our lives, are not eating soundly or sleeping well, or are generally feeling under the weather, the disease agent within us can be activated and the disease will flare up. In other words, when our natural resistance has been lowered by an emotional or environmental stress, our bodies are no longer as effective in warding off disease-causing microbes and we can become ill.

Everyone has areas of his or her body which have a greater susceptibility to disease. You may know families whose members respond to stress through stomach aches, headaches, pollen attacks, or diarrhea. How much of this is learned behavior versus constitution is open to debate. What we do know is that our bodies respond to what is going on in our physical and emotional environments. When we become ill, it can be a signal from our bodies that we have overwhelmed or overstressed our systems. We then have the task of restoring ourselves to good health and exploring what factors led to the illness.

Dr. Thomas H. Holmes, a professor of Psychiatry at the University of Washington, has been a major researcher in the relationship between stress and disease. It is Dr. Holmes' theory that the more a person's major life events change in the period of a year, the greater the likelihood that that person will experience a "health change." A "health change" includes illness, pregnancy, surgery, accidents, and emotional instability. Dr. Holmes' questionnaire will help you determine how many Life Change Units you accumulated during the past year, and predict how many you will accumulate during the next.

You can detect a dangerous sequence of stressful events through the Holmes Schedule of Recent Experiences. The number assigned to each event is a measure of the stress it places on you. Note that many of these events should be happy ones—but change itself may be stressful, even if the change is for the better.

Dr. Holmes' research indicated that 80 percent of persons with scores greater than 300 suffered a serious illness within two years. Fifty-three percent of persons with scores between 250 and 300, and 33 percent of those with scores between 150 and 200, suffered similar illnesses. The ability of the Holmes Scale to predict serious illness demonstrates that unusual stress may be as much a risk to your health as high blood pressure. None of us can entirely avoid stressful situations, but by recognizing the importance of these changes, by trying to make them slowly and carefully whenever possible, we will be able to deal with them more effectively.

Look over the scale and add up your Life Change Units during the last year. Think about the meaning of each of the events and how you feel about them now. Can you think of ways you might have better prepared for or adjusted to these events? Remember, happy, long-awaited events also take a toll; notice that "Vacation" rates 13 points and "Marriage" rates 50.

Check each item that occurred in your life in the last year. Write the given numerical value for each checked item to the left of the item. Add to obtain your total Holmes Score.

1)	☐	100	____	Death of spouse
2)	☐	73	____	Divorce
3)	☐	65	____	Marital separation
4)	☐	63	____	Jail term
5)	☐	63	____	Death of close family member (except spouse)
6)	☐	53	____	Major personal injury or illness
7)	☐	50	____	Marriage
8)	☐	47	____	Fired at work
9)	☐	45	____	Marital reconciliation
10)	☐	45	____	Retirement
11)	☐	44	____	Change in health of family member (not self)
12)	☐	40	____	Pregnancy
13)	☐	39	____	Sex difficulties
14)	☐	39	____	Gain of new family member
15)	☐	39	____	Business readjustment
16)	☐	38	____	Change in financial state
17)	☐	37	____	Death of close friend
18)	☐	36	____	Change to different occupation
19)	☐	35	____	Change in number of arguments with spouse
20)	☐	31	____	Taking on mortgage over $10,000
21)	☐	30	____	Foreclosure of mortgage or loan

You can see that leaving home for the first time adds up to many Life Change Units. This doesn't mean that you shouldn't leave home! It does mean that you should recognize that your system has been or will be stressed. You can better protect yourself by not taking on any extra changes which you can prevent or delay. You can learn to predict how many and what kind of changes kick off illness for you.

Familiarizing yourself with the Life Change Scale and the theory behind it should help you to maintain good physical and emotional health.

Based on Dr. Holmes' Stress Scale, Jackie Schwartz has developed a

22)	☐	29	___	Change in responsibilities at work
23)	☐	29	___	Son or daughter leaving home
24)	☐	29	___	Trouble with in-laws
25)	☐	28	___	Outstanding personal achievement
26)	☐	26	___	Spouse begins or stops work
27)	☐	26	___	Begin or end school
28)	☐	25	___	Change in living conditions
29)	☐	24	___	Change in personal habits (self or family)
30)	☐	23	___	Trouble with boss
31)	☐	20	___	Change in work hours or conditions
32)	☐	20	___	Change in residence
33)	☐	20	___	Change in schools
34)	☐	19	___	Change in recreation
35)	☐	19	___	Change in church activities
36)	☐	18	___	Change in social activities
37)	☐	17	___	Taking on mortgage or loan less than $10,000
38)	☐	16	___	Change in sleeping habits
39)	☐	15	___	Change in number of family get-togethers
40)	☐	13	___	Change in eating habits
41)	☐	13	___	Vacation
42)	☐	12	___	Christmas
43)	☐	11	___	Minor violations of the law

Holmes Scale * Total ___

Relaxation Log ** This Log helps you:
Identify the sources of stress in your life
Detect your body's early warning symptoms of stress overload
Observe how much your tolerance for stress varies
Recognize how much the sources of stress fluctuate
Learn new ways of responding to stress overload

*From Holmes, T. H. and Rahe, R. H.: The Social Readjustment Rating Scale. *Journal of Psychosomatic Research* 11:213–218, 1967.

**Available from Schwartz, 1908 Benecia, Los Angeles, CA 90025.

Beginning _____ Ending _____

		WEEK 1								WEEK 2						
SOURCES OF STRESS	Day															
	Date															
Separation																
Deadlines																
Noise																
Financial concerns																
Overcrowding																
Relocating																
Change in job responsibilities																
Recent death																
Divorce																
Traffic																
Trouble at home																
Trouble at work																
Current events																
Change in living conditions																
Worry too much																
Outstanding personal achievement																
Gaining a new family member																
Loneliness																
Boredom																
Smoking																
Alcohol																
Drugs																
Weight problem																
Handicap																
Illness or personal injury																
COMMON PHYSIOLOGICAL INDICATORS																
Muscular tension																
Digestive difficulties																
Skin eruptions																
Sleeping difficulties																
Stomach pains																
Grinding of teeth																
Circulatory difficulties																
Headache																
Continued physical pain																
Sexual difficulties																
Excessive sweating																
Chest pains																
Difficulty in breathing																
Depression																
Speech difficulties																
High blood pressure																
Hyperactivity																
Increased irritability																
Absence of menstrual period																
Nervous mannerisms																

Discover what methods of relieving stress work best for you
Identify problem areas in your work, home and community life
Determine what steps you can take to reduce stress
We have included a sample of this Relaxation Log which will give you a way of charting your patterns that cause you to feel excessive tension, and find out what you can do about it.

Beginning _____ Ending _____

	WEEK 1				WEEK 2			
Day									
Date									

COMMON STRESS RELIEVERS
Chewing gum
Taking a stretch break
Focussed breathing
Brisk walk
Grooming
Music
Routine Tasks
Stream-of-consciousness writing
Meditation/yoga/prayer
Exercise
Hot bath/jacuzzi/sauna/steam
Nap/Deep relaxation
Working with hands
Cosmetic improvement
Physical labor or workout
Unilateral rage release
Contact with nature
Gardening
Massage
Contact with friend(s)
Entertainment/social interaction
Sexual activity
Counseling

P tomorrow's goals
L for special occasions
A days off
N reviewing long-range goals

On a scale of 1 to 10 rate:
I HAVE DIFFICULTY
being more assertive
being able to "be myself"
making decisions
expressing anger
maximizing my capabilities
finishing "unfinished business"
being on time

I NEED MORE TIME FOR
myself
friends
family
social stimulation
learning/expansiveness

CALMING RESPONSE PROCEDURES
Using a Calming Procedure

Occasions will arise when you will feel better and act more appropriately if you are calm as opposed to anxious. Times when you might want to use these techniques include: waiting to give a speech or talk before a group or class, getting a diagnosis from your doctor, talking with someone about an unpleasant situation or event, etc.

These calming procedures can be used any time you feel you are in a stressful situation and want quick relief. They can be performed while waiting in line, stopping at a red light, walking slowly, at the half-way point of an exam, or almost anywhere you happen to be. If you feel self-conscious doing these publicly, a minute or two spent doing them in a rest room will give the same good rewards.

Instant Calming Procedures (1 to 3 minutes)

— **With arms on chair, rest hands in lap and tighten the muscles in your legs, back and arms. Hold for 3-5 seconds. Release the tension. Relax.**

— **Breathe in slowly through your nose. Exhale through your mouth, and as you breathe out, silently repeat the word "one." Continue the exercise, maintaining a passive attitude.**

— **Allow your body to go completely limp. Deeply relax your entire body as you do this.**

ALCOHOL AND DRUGS

One way young people have been initiated into adult society has been through the use of drugs, usually alcohol. Being able to buy a drink or a bottle is oftentimes the highpoint of turning 18 or 21 depending on the state law. Life has become more complicated for young people as they are now faced with the availability and wide use of illegal drugs.

For some people the addition of wine or a joint of marijuana compliments a special meal or event. Others, depending on their orientation, would consider these additions as unnecessary, immoral, unhealthy, illegal and so on. If you use drugs or alcohol ask yourself the following questions:

Did I feel I needed it?

Did I enjoy it?

What effect is using it having on my life—physically, emotionally, mentally, financially?

What are the legal consequences?

Am I using drugs or alcohol to avoid dealing with serious issues? The use of drugs and alcohol in the life of a person, young or old, needs to be seriously considered and evaluated by the user from time to time.

Used in moderation, alcohol may be helpful in improving circulation, lowering blood pressure and acting as a mild sedative. Used excessively, alcohol effectively destroys countless lives both physically and emotionally. It takes some experimentation to find out how much alcohol your body can tolerate without becoming ill or disoriented. If you do drink, try to do so with friends, in a safe environment and never when you have to drive.

Illegal drugs, marijuana, speed, cocaine, heroin, are familiar, at least by name, to all. While it appears that infrequent use of marijuana is not harmful to physical health all the evidence is not yet in and we probably have much to learn. When marijuana is *needed* to feel good, or when it is used to avoid the pain of working through a problem, then it is being abused and should be considered harmful to your emotional health.

There is considerable evidence that the harder drugs, cocaine, angel's dust, STP, heroin, do cause more permanent physical damage. Because these drugs are illegal they are often of poor quality, the prices are high, and punishment can mean a police record.

Legal drugs, amphetamines and sedatives, are widely available and their usage is abused. If you are prescribed these drugs by a physician we strongly recommend that you find another physician! At the very least have the prescription druggist explain exactly why he or she is making such a recommendation.

WHEN TO SEE A DOCTOR

The majority of young people leaving home for the first time are in prime overall physical condition. These same young adults (aged 18-22) do suffer high incidences of several temporary but debilitating diseases. These include upper respiratory infections, infectious mononucleosis, pelvic inflammatory disease, bladder infections and venereal disease. These are illnesses which need the attention of a physician.

However, everytime a person suffers a runny nose, sore throat, upset stomach, or other minor physical ills there is no need to rush for medical attention. Doctor's offices, clinics, college infirmaries are always crowded with people who have not learned to tell when bed rest, chicken broth, and aspirin are the treatment of choice or when antibiotics and other wonder drugs are truly needed. Sitting in a crowded waiting room when your system is run down and you're feeling awful may make you feel much worse!

It is beyond the scope of this book to recommend treatment for common diseases. We highly recommend the book, *Take Care of Yourself: A Consumer's Guide to Medical Care,* by Doctors Donald M. Vickery and James F. Fries. They diagram 68 common medical problems giving general information, instructions for home care and help in making the decision to seek medical treatment. Probably the most important distinction you can learn is whether your ailment is caused by a virus, bacteria or allergy. A physician can best treat bacterial infections while home remedies work best for a virus or allergy. Vickery and Fries outline the differences in a clear and readable manner.

If you feel uncomfortable treating yourself or if after three days you're not feeling considerably better, by all means see a doctor. But also learn from the experience so that the next time the same symptoms appear you will know how, or if, you can treat yourself.

On the following page you will find a list of common ailments with space for you and your parents to write down treatment methods and over-the-counter remedies found to be effective.

YOUR MEDICAL KIT

For your individual medical kit include:
Aspirin

Cold (decongestant) tablets

An elastic bandage

Bandages

An antiseptic for superficial wounds

Antacid tablets for minor stomach aches

A thermometer

Buy over-the-counter drugs in small amounts as they deteriorate. Do not assume that any product sold without prescription is automatically safe! A pharmacist can be of great help in pointing out which drugs will be most effective for your complaint. Do not use other people's prescriptions without checking carefully with your physician or health service.

FAMILY REMEDIES

Sore Throat_____

_____

_____

Stomach Ache_____

_____

_____

Fever_____

_____

_____

Vomiting_____

_____

_____

Diarrhea_____

_____

_____

Ear Ache_____

_____

_____

Runny Nose_____

_____

_____

Tooth Ache_____

_____

_____

Head Ache_____

_____

_____

Sore Muscles _____

_____
_____
_____

Poison Ivy - Poison Oak _____

_____
_____
_____

Sun Burn _____

_____
_____
_____

Superficial cuts & scratches _____

_____
_____
_____

Superficial burns _____

_____
_____
_____

Dog bites _____

_____
_____
_____

Insect Stings _____

_____
_____
_____

An excellent book to own is *Take Care of Yourself: A Consumer's Guide to Medical Care,* Donald M. Vickery, M.D. and James F. Fries, M.D., Addison-Wesley Publishing Company, Inc., 1976.

THE MEDICAL VISIT

Your time in the doctor's office is very important to you and to your physician for proper treatment. Consider the following points before your visit.

1. Know your individual and family medical history. In the Personal Record section of this book you will find a medical history for yourself, and another noting important information about your parents and grandparents. Ask your parents for help in filling out these records. Now it is up to you to keep them up to date. For your first visit with a physician bring the medical records with you for reference.

2. Be clear about your current medical problem. Write down when the illness started, what part(s) of the body were affected, what treatment, including medication, you have tried, and any thoughts you have as to how the illness came about.

3. Do not hide important information. Some of the activities you have engaged in (drugs, sex, alcohol) may be embarrassing to discuss but they may be directly contributing to your illness. It is important to work with a physician you feel you can trust with your confidences.

4. Be clear about the doctor's recommendations. Patients often leave a doctor's office unclear as to the diagnosis, the expected course of the illness and the doctor's recommendations. There are ways of not letting this happen to you. Have a pad and pencil with you and before going into the appointment write down:

Does this illness have a name?

What causes this illness?

How long should I expect to feel discomfort?

Are there side effects from the medication?

Are there other ways of treating this disease?

What, if any, tests need to be done and why are they needed?

If you doubt your alertness during the medical interview it is helpful to have a friend come with you and take notes as to the doctor's recommendations and answers to your questions.

5. If medication is prescribed, ask what side effects you might expect. Ask that medication be prescribed by the generic rather than brand name, e.g., aspirin, not Bayer's, as this saves money.

6. Getting a second opinion. It is accepted practice that if surgery is recommended the patient will seek a second, sometimes third, medical opinion. If expensive tests are recommended, or if you are not feeling secure in your doctor's advice, it is advisable to seek a second opinion.

You need not hesitate to tell your doctor what you are doing. It is your right to seek a second opinion and your doctor must (and most do quite willingly) send your records to another physician. In these days of medical-legal battles we find doctors encouraging patients to consult another physician before a serious procedure is undertaken.

When you get home from the medical visit be sure to record in your medical records file the date, your complaint, what was done, and what was recommended. Getting in the habit of doing this will be helpful to you in the future as you continue to acquire a medical record. So, while the information is still fresh in your mind, make sure you get it down in a medical records notebook or file specifically set aside for that purpose.

Paying for Your Medical Care

Paying for medical services is handled differently depending on the medical facility and the patient. The following are just some of the many options available.

1. You receive medical treatment from a private physician and pay a fee-for-service. In some offices, if you pay on the day of treatment there is a 10 percent fee reduction.

2. You pay for the private physician treatment and send your bill to your insurance company which reimburses you part of the cost. You may be insured through your work, your parents may still be able to carry you on their policy or you may purchase an insurance policy for yourself.

3. If you are in college and pay for routine health care (coverage which should be listed in the health contract) you would only be charged for extra procedures.

4. You may belong to a Health Maintenance Organization (HMO) either on your own or through your work. You or your company pay a set yearly fee and you are entitled to as many visits as needed, paying a minimal fee for each visit. HMO's also cover testing, pharmacy and hospitalization, but this kind of coverage is extra to the annual fee.

5. An emergency room in a hospital is a good place to know about but expensive to use for routine matters. Emergency room fees tend to be high because they are used to cover the extra-special equipment needed in this service.

6. Each state has somewhat different regulations providing for the medical care of unemployed or underemployed (low paid) workers. Contact your county hospital or county welfare office to find out the regulations in your area. Sometimes the state will pick up part of the medical costs which can be a great help to low-income persons.

7. Free clinics are established to meet certain limited needs, such as family planning, abortion, drug abuse, alcoholism, and venereal disease. Free clinics may ask for, but are not allowed to require, a donation. They are generally hassle-free and serve well in their designated capacity.

8. Public health clinics are established in each state. They can often provide family planning (contraception) services, pre-natal care, immunizations, tuberculosis and diabetes-screening services, and venereal disease services. To locate these clinics in your area, contact your county's Public Health Department.

CONTRACEPTION

Birth Control Methods

Preventing an unwanted pregnancy is part of a person's decision-making process about the way to run his or her life. In 1976, 60 percent of unmarried persons between the ages of 14 and 19 were sexually active before using birth control methods. In this same age group, there is now a startling 1 million pregnancies each year!

You can determine, as part of your own readiness to be sexually active, your willingness to learn about the different forms of birth control and then responsibly select and carefully use the best method for you. **Our Bodies, Ourselves** (see bibliography) has an outstanding, readable and informative chapter on birth control.

Below is a brief overview of the various methods of birth control. For more detailed information, inquire at your campus health center, the county medical center, the local planned parenthood office, or your physician.

The Pill

The pill is the most widely used method for young women. The pill is highly reliable if taken daily as prescribed. Women with a history of high blood pressure, clotting, or diabetes are usually not prescribed the pill. Like all medications, the pill must be prescribed and used under a physician's care. **Never** medicate yourself with a friend's pill!

Condom (prophylactic, rubber)

A condom is a sheath like a balloon worn on the penis during sexual intercourse. The condom prevents the male sperm from entering the vagina and contacting the female egg. When used in conjunction with the woman using foam, the condom can be 95 percent safe. The condom is essential in preventing the spread of venereal disease. Both drug stores and gas stations sell condoms without prescription.

Contraceptive Foam

Contraceptive foam is a chemical mixture. When the foam is inserted into the vagina, it spreads and covers the cervix (mouth of the womb), forming a physical and chemical barrier so that the sperm cannot get through. Contraceptive foam can be bought at drug stores without prescription.

IUD (Intrauterine Device)

The IUD is a contraceptive device, usually made of plastic in one of a variety of shapes, inserted into the uterus by a doctor or medical practitioner. When a woman wants to become pregnant, the device can be removed by a doctor. The IUD is about 98 percent safe for those women who can use it;

however, women who have never been pregnant often are unable to retain the device.

Diaphragm

The diaphragm is made of soft rubber in the shape of a shallow cup. It has a flexible metal spring rim. It fits snugly over the woman's cervix, locked in place behind the pubic bone and reaching back behind the cervix. It must be fitted to each person by a physician or nurse practitioner. A diaphragm must always be used with spermicidal cream or jelly which can be bought over the counter at the drug store. The diaphragm is perfectly safe. It does not affect the woman's fertility at all. Simply don't use it if you want to become pregnant. Failures do occur about 2 percent of the time even when the diaphragm is properly used. The diaphragm can be combined with a condom on fertile days, increasing the effectivenes of the diaphragm.

ABORTION

The termination of a pregnancy is considered an abortion. An abortion may occur spontaneously, which is nature's way of dealing with an unhealthy fetus. Abortions performed by the pregnant woman or non-medically trained persons are dangerous to the woman, as the uterus can be permanently damaged, hemorrhaging may be severe, and the risk of infection is great. Abortion is safest if performed by a trained medical practitioner under sterile conditions when the pregnancy is no more than 20, and preferably 12 to 16 weeks along.

In January, 1973, the U.S. Supreme court made abortion legally possible for any woman in the country under certain circumstances:

During the first 3 months of pregnancy, any woman can have an abortion performed by a licensed physician. The decision to abort is between the woman and her physician and is a medical decision.

During the second 3 months, the State may specify under what sanitary conditions an abortion may be accomplished, but may not interfere in any other manner.

During the last 3 months, the State may (but is not required to) prohibit abortion unless the woman's life or health is endangered by the pregnancy. It is unusual to perform an abortion after the sixth month because it then becomes a dangerous operation.

Abortion clinics and services vary from state to state, and even within states. So, while abortion is legal, it is not always easily come by. Furthermore, in the years since 1973, there has been mounting protest against the Supreme Court decision, and it seems likely that this issue will go through the courts again in the next few years.

You may have to do some searching for an abortion clinic. Call your local planned parenthood office or check with the various heath agencies in your city to find out what their services are. Since the cost of an abortion can vary considerably, make sure you inquire about the cost. Medical insurance policies sometimes cover it. Above all, it is most important that you get services from well-trained medical persons and, if possible, that you have the abortion before the pregnancy is 12 weeks along. (The pregnancy test can reveal nothing until at least 10 days after your period was due.) At this stage, the procedure is a simple, and often painless one.

Early Abortion - First Trimester

Up to 12 weeks the usual procedure is to open the womb and insert a small tube through the cervix. By suction, the womb is gently emptied of the embryo.

Dilation and Currettage (D & C)

The opening of the womb is dilated and the uterus is cleaned with a currette. This is done during the first trimester.

Menstrual Extraction or Endrometrial Aspiration

A tube or syringe is inserted through the cervix into the uterus and gently sucks out the tissue from the wall of the uterus. This is done during the first two weeks after a menstrual period is missed.

Late Abortion - Second Trimester

After 16 weeks of pregnancy, amniotic fluid is withdrawn and a saline (salt) solution is injected into the sac surrounding the fetus. The cervix dilates and the fetus and placenta are expelled. This type of abortion can be as painful as childbirth, and carries some risk.

Whether or not to terminate a pregnancy is often a difficult decision. Even those who are sure they do want to terminate the pregnancy report feeling some conflict, anger and sadness. It is strongly advised that as soon as you think you might be pregnant, schedule a lab pregnancy test. If the test is positive (which means you are pregnant), you still have several weeks (4-6) to make your decision. In all major cities and also in many smaller communities, there are counseling services to help women (and men, if the women want them to participate) look at the alternatives and come to their own decision.

The sexually active person who is acting responsibly knows there is a risk of pregnancy, since birth control methods are not 100 percent efffective. In light of this fact, some thought should be given about the possibilities of what to do about an unwanted pregnancy.

ADOPTION

If you decide you do not want to terminate your pregnancy and that you also do not want to, or do not feel able to, keep your baby, you can place the baby for adoption. This means that you would relinquish all rights and responsibilities as a parent. Either an agency, a doctor, or a lawyer would place the child with a couple who want a child but are unable to complete their own pregnancy.

Working with a good adoption agency offers you the opportunity to look at your decision and to know that the agency will have high standards in placing your child in a family that can offer the love and care which is every child's birthright.

For further information on adoption, call the adoptive unit of your county welfare department, the Catholic, Jewish or Protestant Family Service Agency in your area, or speak with your doctor about adopting services.

KEEPING YOUR BABY

You may decide not to terminate your pregnancy, but to deliver and keep your baby. This is an enormous decision! You are making a commitment to being responsible for another person for the next 18 years. If you are under age 22, this probably means that you are left without a full education or career training which then may result in your spending many years being financially dependent on your parents or on the welfare sysem. Certainly people have done it before, and it is possible to raise a child and go back to school, but it is a big decision and a major responsibility, and it will radically change your way of life.

There is a growing trend for unmarried women in their 30's to choose to have a child. It is important that you realize that there is over ten years of life experience between these women and the young adults to whom this book is addressed.

Every woman who decides to bring a child into the world needs to find and follow good medical care, needs emotional support from friends and family, and needs financial support during the latter part of pregnancy and at least during the first months after delivery. Look to your county welfare department, county health agency, and private family service agencies for whatever supportive programs they may offer. Sometimes the Red Cross and adult education programs in the schools offer preparation for childbirth classes, pre-natal exercise classes and support groups.

VENEREAL DISEASE

What is VD?

Venereal disease is the general name given to those diseases caused by organisms which are passed directly from person to person during sexual relations. The two venereal diseases that are the most damaging to physical health are syphilis and gonorrhea. They are two different diseases caused by two different germs. It is possible to be infected with both syphilis and gonorrhea at the same time.

How do you Catch VD?

Syphilis and gonorrhea are transmitted from person to person by sexual intercourse or by close body contact involving the sex organs, mouth, or rectum.

How Do You Prevent VD?

The only sure way to avoid venereal diseases is to avoid intimate contact with persons who are infected. Use of soap and water and the condom can prevent spread from one infected person to another.

What Ways Can You Treat VD?

Treatment time may vary from several days to two weeks. Cure is possible at any stage of the disease, but medication cannot restore damaged tissues. Only a doctor can diagnose and prescribe the proper medicine. DO NOT USE OTHERS' MEDICINE OR HOME REMEDIES.

Symptoms of Gonorrhea in the Male

The disease begins with a painful inflammation of the urethra (the center of the penis) two to six days after exposure to an infected person. If this occurs, go to a doctor or health clinic immediately.

Symptoms of Gonorrhea in the Female

Most often, there are no immediate symptoms. Pain in the stomach and fever may result, with damage to the reproductive organs. Early medical treatment is advisable; hospitalization may be necessary. Pelvic inflammatory disease may also be caused by organisms other than gonorrhea.

Symptoms of Syphilis in Males and Females

Symptoms of syphilis are difficult to notice. Early signs include a rash or painless sores (chancres). Both the rash and sores go away after a few days even without treatment, but that should not be taken as an indication that the disease has gone away. It only means that you cannot see the symptoms. Treatment is still needed. If treatment is not obtained, syphilis has very serious consequences including blindness and death.

Herpes II Virus

Herpes II is a painful viral disease which has recently reached epidemic proportions. It is estimated that over 30 percent of the sexually active population in the United States is now infected.

Herpes II is known as "genital herpes." It should not be confused with Herpes I which causes cold sores or fever blisters affecting the eyes, lips, skin, or inside of the throat. However, Herpes II infections occur most commonly in persons who experienced Herpes I infections during childhood.

In Herpes II, fluid-filled sores or blisters appear on the inside of the vagina, on the external genitals, on the penis, thighs, in or near the anus, and on the buttocks. The condition is most infectious—and most painful—when the blisters rupture. After 4-5 days the sores become less painful and begin to heal by themselves.

While there is no known cure for Herpes II it is recommended that medical treatment be followed for relief of symptoms and complications. Persons with Herpes II infections should be examined once or twice a week until the sores disappear. Infected females, as well as uninfected females who have had sexual intercourse with a man who has had Herpes II, should have a PAP test twice a year on a regular basis.

It is thought that once a person has contracted Herpes II the virus remains in the system and subsequent attacks are triggered by sunlight, general poor health, emotional stress, and possibly even certain foods and drugs. Look for new findings on the treatment of Herpes II in the future.

What Should I Do if I Think I Have VD?

If you are a sexually active person and think that your partner is having sexual relations with someone other than you, it is important to have a check-up for VD every three months.

What Does a Check-up Consist Of?

At the health clinic or your doctor's office, they check for gonorrhea with a swab of fluid from a woman's cervix and from the fluid from the tip of a man's penis. Syphilis is checked in the male and female through a blood test, commonly known as a Wasserman test.

Is the Information Confidential?

Yes. Statistics on the diseases the doctor or clinic is treating may be sent to a state health agency, but information about **you** is kept absolutely confidential.

PSYCHOLOGICAL COUNSELING

The task of a counselor is to listen, to provide a safe environment for exploring fears and concerns and to facilitate your coping with stress in a way that allows you to go on with your job or schooling in the most comfortable and productive way.

It's an outdated myth that a person is crazy or weak if he or she needs counseling. Oftentimes, a few counseling sessions can put a current problem in perspective and can alleviate emotional distress. More lengthy counseling may be necessary for problems that are more complex. Sometimes feelings of discomfort are transitory and will disappear as you feel more familiar in your new surroundings. However, it is not uncommon for the discomfort to continue and get in the way of your success. At that point, the best course of action is to find professional help. Places to begin looking include: a university medical service; a minister, rabbi or priest; county departments of mental health services; and private counselors or therapists.

Emotional stress is inevitable as long as we are fully alive and engaged in pursuing studies, work and relationships. Colleges and more-progressive businesses are aware of the stress in adapting to a new environment and new challenges. They employ counselors (clinical social workers, psychologists and psychiatrists) to help students or employees deal more effectively with their personal lives. What goes on between the counselor and the person requesting help is strictly confidential.

CHOOSING A COUNSELOR

There are a wide variety of counseling services available in or near most communities. Some of these are college or university health services, county departments of mental health, private agencies, family service, and social service agencies, some sponsored by religious denominations. Private practice counselors are listed in the Yellow Pages of your phone directory under Marriage and Family Counselors, Psychologists, Clinical Social Workers, and Psychiatrists. Another resource for counseling is the HELP or CRISIS Line. These telephone numbers can often be found in laundromats, phone booths and coffee shops frequented by young adults.

You may have to do some phoning around before you find a place that sounds like it has the kind of service you are looking for. Make an appointment and note how the receptionist responds to you and to other clients and how you feel in this setting.

When you sit down with a counselor, be aware of how you feel with this person. Ask yourself these questions: Am I being listened to? Are my feelings taken seriously? Do I think I can be honest with this counselor?

Remember, it takes awhile to get to know and to feel free to open up to a new person. Counselors are skilled in helping you open up without great discomfort. Counseling may also help you to learn about and handle your own rhythm and inner time table.

If, after a few visits (3-5), you still don't feel the fit between you and the counselor is good, it's important that you talk about this directly with your counselor. This is a time when people often pull out of therapy because it is frightening to tell authority figures you are not pleased with their work. Exploring the difficulties can turn out to be a powerful experience. This may be the first time you have questioned an adult and have not been responded to with anger, punishment, defensiveness, or tears. You may end up knowing what it feels like to deal with someone as adult-to-adult. After the air has cleared, you and the counselor may mutually decide to continue treatment or that a referral would be in your best interests.

Before calling for an appointment, ask yourself:

What do I want—information, help through a crisis period, or long-term counseling?

Do I want anyone else, such as my family, boy/girlfriend, roommate, to participate with me?

Does it make a difference to me if I work with a male or female counselor?

What is my financial ability? Think about whether your parents would help with the fee, or if you are still covered by their insurance. Ask if the agency or individual practitioner has a sliding fee scale, and if so, whether you would be eligible.

RIGHTS AND RESPONSIBILITIES
AS A CLIENT

Your Rights as a Client:

1. The right to confidentiality between you and your counselor.

2. The right to change therapists.

3. To be treated with respect.

4. To be listened to seriously. This is not a social situation, but a time to work on what you need to work on.

5. To decide whether or not you will follow your counselor's advice. Your counselor may decide that if certain advice is not followed, he or she does not wish to continue working with you.

6. The right to your own feelings, even if they do not agree with those of the therapist.

7. The right to ask for the emotional support you need. Your counselor may not believe support is in your best interest and it may be denied.

Your Responsibilities as a Client:

1. To be as honest and open with yourself and your counselor as you are able to be.

2. To keep your appointments and to be on time. Make sure you understand the therapist's guidelines on cancelling appointments, vacation time, illness, etc.

3. It is your responsibility to pay the agreed upon fee at the agreed upon time unless you and the therapist can work out a different arrangement.

WORK AND
CAREER PLANNING

"Doctor, Lawyer, Indian Chief"

There is a big difference between a job and a career. Most of you have held jobs already, doing yard work, pumping gas, stock and sales work, bagging in a grocery store, filling orders at quick-stop food outlets, etc. Many of you will continue to do these kinds of jobs to earn money as you pursue your studies or acquire more advanced on-the-job training for a career. These jobs have earned you money and they have also taught you about what kinds of working situations you like best (and least) and do well (or poorly) in.

The information and checklists in this section are designed to help you find a job you like that can possibly further your career goals. Fill out the resume, the work history and job reaction forms and you will probably begin to get insight into the kind of career you want to head for. You will also find a check-list on occupations which is another aid for helping you, and perhaps a career counselor can help you to develop a better picture of your strengths and aptitudes.

In this chapter you will find material that will prepare you for the types of questions a potential employer may ask. Thinking through your answers in advance of the interview will help you to be more at ease and to come across in a stronger manner. There is also a checklist for reasons why you might not have been hired. Studying this and honestly thinking about your presentation during the interview may alert you so that you do not repeat the same mistakes in future interviews.

In recent years, there have been both legislation and new employment laws. You will find a review of the most important of these new laws in this chapter. Make a copy of the resume and work history forms and keep these up to date. Save yourself time and energy by taking a copy of your filled out application form to potential employers.

JOB AND CAREER

Very few people graduate from high school knowing exactly what kind of work they want to do. Even if you know your general area of interest—let's say business or law—you may be confused by or unaware of the many options for working in your chosen field.

It used to be that people studied for a career and pursued that career—perhaps for different companies and in new cities—until retirement. Now, it is not unusual to hear of people in their 40's and 50's re-entering school and starting out in new careers. This happens sometimes because there are changes in the job market and sometimes because each of us changes, and we develop new interests and want to expand our skills and explore new areas.

When thinking about career and jobs, it's important to consider your likes and dislikes, your skills, interests, and aptitudes. What interests you, how might you be able to combine your hobby and your career, do you like to work indoors or out, with people or alone, with your body or your mind?

There are career counselors who you may consult. A career counselor can administer and interpret vocational tests which define your special aptitudes; your special needs; advise you of current and long-range job market trends; and know the best schools or training programs in your field.

Most colleges and universities have a career counseling department. Adult school programs, the Employment Development Department in your county, and the Department of Vocational Rehabilitation (for physically and emotionally handicapped) also offer career counseling. The forms on the following pages will be helpful to you in focusing on career goals.

1.
Name of Employer _____ Address _____

Position _____ Name of Supervisor _____ Salary _____

2.
Name of Employer _____ Address _____

Position _____ Name of Supervisor _____ Salary _____

3.
Name of Employer _____ Address _____

Position _____ Name of Supervisor _____ Salary _____

Social Security Number _____ (You must obtain a card before going to work)

Two Business People Who Would Recommend Me.

1.
Name _____ Address _____ Type of Business _____

2.
Name _____ Address _____ Type of Business _____

Type of Job I would Like Right Now: _____

My Long Term Career Goal is _____

Ways I have planned to achieve this goal: (for example, part-time jobs, full-time jobs) _____

School (Adult, Vocational, College) _____

_____

_____

PERSONAL RESUME

Name_____Social Security No._____

Address_____|_____Phone_____

Type of Position Sought:_____

Experience:_____

_____

_____

Education:_____

_____

_____

Honors:_____

_____

_____

Outside Activities:_____

_____

_____

Volunteer Work:_____

_____

_____

Foreign Languages Read or Spoken:_____

_____

_____

Salary:_____

_____

_____

References: (3 former employers or business people who know you.)

1._____
     (Name)   (Address)   (City)   (Phone)

2._____

3._____

When applying for some jobs, along with the application form they may ask you to send in a resume. These are some of the types of items that you might include in your resume to them. It is a good idea to keep this record up-to-date as your skills and jobs expand.

JOB REACTION FORM

Think about the various jobs you have had and complete the form. What will emerge may be interesting information for you.

Job Tasks I especially like:

   1. _____

   2. _____

   3. _____

Job Tasks I dislike:

   1. _____

   2. _____

   3. _____

My on-the-job strengths:

   1. _____

   2. _____

   3. _____

My on-the-job weaknesses:

   1. _____

   2. _____

   3. _____

Supervisors' reactions to me and my work:

1. _____
2. _____
3. _____

In what areas would I like more skills:

1. _____
2. _____
3. _____

RESOURCES FOR FINDING A JOB

Employment Development Department (EDD)_____

Phone

Department of Vocational Rehabilitation_____

Civil Service (Government Jobs)   Personnel Office Addresses:

City_____

State_____

County_____

Federal_____

Local Colleges/Universities_____

_____

Newspapers_____

Unions (AFL, etc.)_____

Friends - This is the most common way of finding a job. Make a list of your friends and check with them about job possibilities.

1._____
2._____

3._____

4._____

Private Employment Agencies - Some are free for the employee; others charge a fee to the job seeker. Check this out. Try other resources first, but in a tight job market, it may be worth it in the long run to pay an agency for placing you in a job.

Bulletin Boards - at schools, supermarkets, apartment complexes

Calling Directly: Go to a store or business that you know about and ask if they have any openings. Be specific about what you can offer them.

A Checklist of Facts You Should Know
When Considering an Occupation

*Occupation I'm considering:*_____

	YES	NO
1. Are workers in this occupation in demand at present?	____	____
2. Will workers in this occupation be in demand in the future?	____	____
3. Is overtime or shift work required?	____	____
4. Will I be required to use a lot of physical energy such as stooping, crawling, kneeling, balancing, pushing, finger dexterity, etc.?	____	____
5. Will I be required to work with machines, tools?	____	____
6. Does the work require a great deal of competitiveness?	____	____
7. Will I have a lot of responsibility?	____	____

8. Is the work environment hot, cold, humid, dry, noisy, windy? _____ _____

9. Are there many hazards in the job, such as electric shock, vibrations, explosives, poisoned air, etc.? _____ _____

10. Will I be required to work in cramped quarters, high places? _____ _____

11. Is there a lot of precision and pressure on this job? _____ _____

12. Is the job repetitive? _____ _____

13. Will I have freedom to come and go as I wish? _____ _____

14. Will I be directly serving others? _____ _____

15. Will I be able to use my creativity, initiative and judgment? _____ _____

16. Is there an opportunity to be a leader? _____ _____

17. Are there upper & lower age limits for getting into the job? _____ _____

18. Do I have the proper education for this job? _____ _____

19. Do I need city, state or federal licensing or certification for this job? _____ _____

20. Must I be a citizen of the United States? _____ _____

21. Do I have to live within the city or state in order to have the job? _____ _____

22. Do I need special tools, supplies, uniforms, vehicles (truck)? _____ _____

23. Do I need to be a member of a union? _____ _____

24. Does vacation time and pay come with the job? _____ _____

25. Can I earn seniority? _____ _____

26. Are there opportunities for advancement? _____ _____

27. Does the job provide social prestige? _____ _____

28. Do I want social prestige? _____ _____

29. Will I have time for my schooling, hobbies, and recreation? _____ _____

30. Is housing available within a reasonable distance?   _____   _____

31. Can I afford the housing in the area?   _____   _____

32. Is there adequate transportation and commuter service?   _____   _____

33. Does the climate appear satisfactory?   _____   _____

34. Are there schools available for further training?   _____   _____

Look over your answers to these questions. Are there parts of this occupation that do not appeal to you?_____

Which parts don't you like?_____

_____

Do you still think you want to go into this occupation?_____
If not, there are over 25,000 more occupations to choose from. Do not be discouraged. Xerox this checklist and go over it for each occupation you are considering.

REMEMBER—THIS IS YOUR LIFE. CHOOSE A JOB OR PROFESSION THAT PLEASES YOU!

RESEARCHING THE EMPLOYER
(Before the Interview)

Each company likes to think of themselves as the best in their field. They are so involved with themselves that if you don't know about them, they think there is something wrong with you! If the company is located away from your present home, find out something about the new community. The employer will be interested in your ability to adjust to a new locale.

What does the firm do?_____

How old is the company or how long has it been in business?

_____

Where are its plants, stores, offices?_____

What are its products or services?_____

What has been its growth?_____

How does its prospects for the future look?_____

Does the company's product or service have a long-term market?

_____

Who is in charge of the company?_____
Who is in charge of the department you would be working for?

_____

Who are the competitors?_____
How many in the field?_____
Are they large or small?_____
What are the company's financial prospects?_____

_____

What are firm's services/products/distinctions?_____

_____

What kinds of jobs do they have that I could do?_____

_____

Research your employer so carefully and thoroughly that you can second guess what the hiring criteria are apt to be.

If it is out of your local area, the employer will be curious about your ability to adjust to the new environment. Know something about the area as well as the job.

THE SIXTEEN MOST-ASKED QUESTIONS
IN THE INTERVIEW

Don't walk into an interview without thinking through the answers to these sixteen most-asked questions

1. **In what type of position are you most interested?**

2. **Why do you think you would like to work for our company?**

3. What jobs have you held, how were they obtained, and why did you leave?

4. What do you know about our company?

5. What would you do if . . . ? (They would ask about a situation that might happen on the job.)

6. What are your ideas on salary?

7. Why do you think you would like this particular job?

8. Can you get recommendations from previous employers?

9. What interests you about our product or service?

10. Are you looking for a permanent or a temporary job?

11. How long do you expect to work?

12. Are you willing to go where the company sends you? ____

13. What are your own special abilities?

14. What kind of work interests you?

15. Why should we hire YOU for this job, rather than anyone else?

16. How did you find out about this job?

Your answers to these questions are important; however, HOW you answer them are many times even more important. It is helpful to keep in mind a few interpersonal skills in the interview, such as:

1. Look at your interviewer when you listen to and answer his/her questions.

2. If you don't know the answer to a question, be honest.

3. If a handshake is offered, give a firm shake—not a limp, "dead fish" handshake.

4. Only smoke during the interview if the interviewer asks if you want to smoke. Don't chew gum!

5. Dress appropriately for the interview. If you're unsure about what is appropriate, spend some time in the area of the job (i.e., the lobby of the building) and note what those already employed are wearing.

6. Never complain about your previous bosses. Your new boss won't like the idea that you might complain about them in your next job interview.

7. Don't slump or slouch in your chair. Sit comfortably without fussing or fidgeting.

8. Keep your answers short and to the point.

9. Body language is important. Smile when appropriate and if you can, help the interviewer feel comfortable with you.

REASONS FOR NOT BEING HIRED

Employers are in business to make a profit, or, like government and voluntary agencies, to provide a service. They want an employee who will help them reach their goal. The best person to hire is the one who will cost the least to train and supervise and who has the greatest potential for advancing within the organization. Some reasons why you may not be hired include:

1. **Lack of planning for a career—no purpose or goal**

2. **Lack of interest and enthusiasm—passive, indifferent**

3. **Lack of confidence and poise—nervous, ill at ease**

4. Never heard of the company and no interest in the company

5. Poor personal appearance

6. Overbearing, too aggressive, conceited, superiority complex, "know it all"

7. Inability to express self clearly—poor voice, diction, grammar

8. Overemphasis on money, interest only in best dollar offer

9. Poor scholastic record (barely passing grades) and showing a marked dislike for school

10. Unwilling to start at the bottom; expects too much too soon

11. Making excuses, hedging on unfavorable factors in record, evasive

12. Lack of courtesy, ill-mannered

13. Condemnation of past employers

14. Failure to look interviewer in the eye

15. Limp, "dead fish" handshake

16. Sloppy application blank

17. Wanting job only for short time

18. Lack of knowledge in field of specialization

19. Parents make decision

20. Emphasis on whom she knows—(name dropping)

21. Unwillingness to go where sent

22. Poor handling of personal finances

23. Inability to take criticism

24. Late to interview without good reason

25. Asking no questions about the job

26. Indefinite response to questions

QUESTIONS AN EMPLOYER IS NOT LEGALLY ENTITLED TO ASK

The following are questions a potential employer may not ask of you. Under the Fair Employment Practices Act, you are not required to answer or to comply, and, in fact, you can sue the company for asking these questions.

KNOW YOUR RIGHTS

1. They may not ask you about the ancestry, lineage, national origin or your descent, based on your name.

2. They may not ask if you are married, single, divorced, engaged. Nor may they ask the number and/or age of children you have or if you are pregnant.

3. They may not require that you produce proof of age in the form of a birth certificate or baptismal record. You may, however, be expected to submit proof of age in the form of a birth certificate *after* being hired.

4. They may not ask about any handicaps which do not relate to your fitness to perform the job.

5. Your sex cannot be used as a factor for determining whether or not you can handle a job.

6. Your race, color of your skin, eyes, hair, etc., or other questions directly or indirectly indicating race or color may not be asked. Your height or weight is not allowed to be questioned if it is not relevant to the job.

7. Questions about the person with whom you live are not permitted.

8. Questions about your birthplace, the birthplace of your parents, spouse or other relatives are not permitted.

9. They may not request a photograph before hiring you.

10. If you were in the military service, the type of discharge you received need not be divulged.

11. Questions such as "Of what country are you a citizen?" or "Are your parents naturalized or native-born U.S. citizens?" are not allowed.

12. Questions about the nationality, racial or religious aspects of a school you attended, or your first language, or how your foreign language ability was acquired are illegal.

13. Any questions relating to arrests, court appearances, or conviction record, if not directly related to the functions and responsibilities of the job, are illegal.

14. An adult applicant can refuse to answer questions regarding the name or address of any relative, even for an emergency.

15. You need not supply any information about organizations, clubs, societies and lodges to which you belong.

16. You need not answer questions concerning your credit rating, charge accounts, or other financial information.

17. You need not submit religious references or references from your pastor or rabbi.

If these questions are asked during an interview, you may answer them if you wish. However, you may tell the interviewer that you know the questions are no longer legal and that you do not wish to respond. You may decide to add that if the interviewer could tell you more about the reason for wanting the information, you could then decide whether to answer.

Refusing to answer these questions could make it appear that you are a trouble-maker and you may lose out on the job. On the other hand, the interviewer may see you as an aware person who is not easily intimidated. How the interviewer responds to your statements also gives you an indication of how this company respects the law and the rights of its employees.

If you decide to press charges against the company, call the Equal Employment Opportunity Commission in your state for further information.

EMPLOYMENT LAWS

Employment laws have been changing rapidly over the past few years. If you believe that your employer or a prospective employer is not complying with the law, you can make inquiries to any of these resources:

1. Equal Employment Opportunity Commission

2. Fair Employment Practices Commission

3. U.S. Department of Labor, Wages and Hours Division

4. A private attorney (one with expertise in labor and discrimination laws)

5. Certain groups like the Urban League, The National Organization of Women, The American Civil Liberties Union, have task forces set up to help persons who are discriminated against in work situations.

If it turns out that you are correct—that your employer has been acting illegally—the above agencies are available in helping you either to negotiate with or bring a suit against your employer.

The following are some of the new laws pertaining to women. They are just a small sample of laws affecting employment.

It is against the law:

— to refuse to hire a woman merely because she is a woman.

— to pay women employees wages and benefits different from those paid to male employees for substantially the same work.

— not to offer women employees an equal chance for advancement through systems of promotion and transfer.

— to fire a woman employee merely because she is a woman.

— for an employer, advertising agency or union to advertise ONLY for male job applicants unless being male is absolutely necessary in order to perform the job.

— for employment agencies to refer only some qualified applicants.

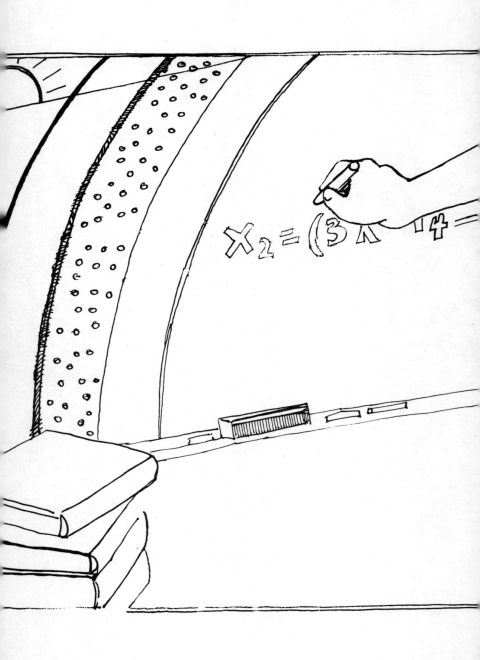

SCHOOL

High school graduation marks the beginning for young adults to go off in different directions. By far the most travelled direction will be going on to school so as to train and acquire the skills needed for a career, a vocation, or a profession. In this section we briefly describe the different kinds of schools, technical, vocational, liberal arts, from which to choose.

We have included a discussion of the application process, of how schools select students, and of ways to finance your education. Lastly, we offer a dozen tips on how to make it in academia.

When you entered high school you designed your high school academic program, hopefully along with your counselor and your parents, having in mind the general kind of training you would later pursue. Of course, at age 14 you might not have known what you wanted to prepare for, or where your special interests lay, or in what fields you had special aptitudes. But, you probably knew whether you'd be heading for college or for vocational school. Before you can go on to whatever training you now choose it might mean that you need additional course work in the subject areas that had not been in your original program. Stick it out; remember, you're preparing yourself for your future work career and a few extra months at this end can mean years of difference later on.

TYPES OF SCHOOLS

There are many types of schools to attend to further your career: Technical Schools, i.e. secretarial, barbering, hair dressing. Vocational Programs (sometimes in junior or community colleges) i.e. nursing, police science, dental hygiene, restaurant management. Community College (AA degree, 2 years) students may go on to a 4 yr. college or university. State College or University (B.A. or B.S. degree) students may go on to graduate programs. Private college or University (B.A. or B.S. degree) students may go on to graduate programs. State or Private Professional Schools (Law, Medicine, Business, Social Work, Library Science, Engineering, etc.) These schools one attends after completing a Bachelor's Degree.

Two other important sources for training are 1) large corporations (IBM, General Motors, banks) many of which have their own extensive training programs and, 2) the Armed Services (U.S. Army, Navy, Coast Guard, Air Force and Marine Corps). Both of these sources provide you with on-going jobs (and an income) and training in areas that can advance your career.

The Application Process

Make sure you have an up-to-date catalog of the schools you are applying to so that you can be sure you have the exact requirements and dates. Catalogs are usually available in your high school counseling offices, at the public library or directly from the schools themselves. When you send for a catalog directly from the school, there is usually a few dollars' handling charge.

Make a chart showing **what** schools need **what** information and by **when.**

Apply to more than one college. Even if you have always wanted to go to your mom's school, it makes sense not to put all your eggs in one basket. If you are not admitted to your first-choice school, you will then have others to fall back on. If after a year or two you still want to go to a certain school, you can reapply and have your application for admission reviewed again.

Entrance Procedures

1. Give your high school at least one month's lead time to get your transcript out to the college(s) you are applying to.
2. Take the time to write legibly, or, preferably, type your application.
3. Ask for help from your counselor, teachers and parents if you do not understand all the questions on the application form.
4. Make sure your application is in by the deadline date. The sooner, the better.
5. After you have been accepted, make sure you reply whether or not you will be attending by the date requested.

If the college(s) of your choice requires the Scholastic Aptitude Test (SAT) or the American College Testing Program (ACT), find out from your high school counselor when and where these tests are to be given. You must sign up and pay for the tests several weeks before they are administered. Register for these tests as soon as you can; frequently a given testing center will "close up" as names pour in.

It is best to take the college boards more than once. First of all, you can get a sense of what is on them; secondly, you can have your scores averaged.

It's a good idea to take the tests at the end of your junior year and then once or twice as a senior. Most colleges prefer that you take your SAT's before February 1st of your senior year. Many bookstores and libraries have study guides in preparing for these examinations. They offer sample questions, answers and tips for taking the tests.

The Selection Process

Matching the right student to the right school is a difficult task. By applying you are making a statement that you believe you could benefit from the program and be a positive force in the community. The school then has to examine your file and determine if they too believe you would be successful in the program they offer. It is expensive, both financially and emotionally to you, and financially to the school, not to pick wisely.

The criteria used by colleges and universities in the selection of students vary, but the following are the major factors, ranked in order of their importance, considered by admissions committees in private colleges and universities as well as in some state-supported universities.

Rank in high school classes
Grade Point Average
Scores on the Scholastic Aptitude Test of the College Board
Scores on the Achievement Tests of the College Board
Recommendations from your high school counselor or principal and from two teachers
Participation in extracurricular activities
Prizes of distinction won in any field
Work or volunteer experience

In addition, admissions committees may also give more weight to your application if either one of your parents or a sibling attended the school. This is also true if you are recommended by an alumni group.

A personal interview, though often not feasible because of distance, is helpful in that it permits applicants to learn more about the college than what appears in the bulletin, and allows the admissions committee to learn more about the student than can be learned from the application form. Students choosing to have an interview should be prepared to talk informally about their academic record, interests, talents, and goals.

FINANCING YOUR EDUCATION

Everyone is aware of the high cost of continuing education. Some students may decide to put off going on to school for a year or so while they work and earn money; others decide to live at home and attend a community college during the first two years; others take a light program and work during school. If you are really serious about wanting to go on in school there is probably some way you can find to do it.

Your high school counselor should be the first person you contact to find out about the various financial aid resources. But your counselor may not know all the resources so it is important for you to do something in your own behalf.

1. Write to the college(s) you're considering and find out about their scholarship, aid, loan, or work-study program.

2. Write to your state congressman and find out what financial aid programs your state may have for encouraging advanced education.

3. Talk with your local banker about low-interest educational loans. Such loans are federally backed; payments (as low as $30.00 per month) are to start after college graduation and can extend out to ten years.

4. Call the Federal Student Information Center, toll-free 1-800-638-6700 for information about financial aid programs financed by the federal government.

5. Send for the following free pamphlets:
   Guide for Parents and Students, American College Testing Program, Box 168, Iowa City, Iowa, 52243.

   Meeting College Costs, College Scholarship Service, 888 Seventh Ave., New York 10019.

   The Student Consumer's Guide: Six Federal Financial Aid Programs, Basic Grant, Box 84, Washington, D.C., 20043.

It is our understanding that innumerable grants go unused year after year. Sometimes this is because the donor has asked that the grantee be of such specific dimensions (female nursing candidate with both French and Indian background) that it is difficult to find the person; sometimes the money sits because no one has sought it out. Filling out forms for aid is bothersome but it is usually well worth the effort.

SOME TIPS FOR MAKING IT IN ACADEMIA

Many students find college considerably more difficult than high school. The work may also be much more interesting and challenging and you may be delighted with B's and C's where you had formerly only known A's. Below you will find some tips for helping you to succeed in academia.

Be There. You may believe that you can learn all you need by reading the assignments and by doing well on the tests. If you are in a small class you are missing the opportunity of getting to know the professor. It is also true that some professors feel angry or hurt when a student doesn't attend class and some make it a point to lower a student's grade even if the exam shows knowledge of the subject matter.

Look Alert. Teachers like to believe that their class and their presentation of the material is interesting, especially if the class is in the teacher's area of expertise. She is unlikely to be pleased with students who are obviously bored or disinterested in the subject matter. Alert eyes, a nod of your head, a smile, note taking,are all ways in which you indicate that you are really there, alert and interested.

Don't be afraid to show your ignorance. It's most likely true that if you don't understand something there's someone else in the class that doesn't understand either. Make an educated guess but make sure you understand the reasoning behind the answer. On the other hand, the "know-it-all" student is a pain in the neck to teachers and to other students and is best dealt with firmly.

Be aware of what is important to your professor. In the first few meetings of the class the professor will tell how much weight is put on class participation, papers, exams, projects, etc. Listen for what types of tests will be given, how often, expectations for reading beyond the text. Clue in to the professor's tone of voice and non-verbal body messages to find out what is of special importance.

Follow instructions. If you hand in your work just the way you want to, not the way instructed, you are sure to lose grade points. Listen to what is asked for and follow the instructions.

Watch details. Be careful to check over math problems, to look up words you might be misspelling and grammar which is incorrect. Your ideas may be creative but you will not get full credit if your work is sloppy.

Show intellectual curiosity. Creative and secure teachers enjoy having students who point out the holes in theories, who question, who make up their own examples of the concepts being taught. You show your teacher that you are interested in the work by doing extra reading and by coming by during office hours to discuss what you are learning and to have the teacher direct you deeper into the subject matter.

Participate in Class. If the class is a large lecture then you participate best by looking alert and asking questions during the question time. If the class is a small seminar it is expected that you will participate with ideas as well as questions. Your involvement in the class will determine part of your grade but more importantly it will determine how much you get out of the course.

Write legibly. We know you've heard it before but it's still true; when a teacher has many papers to read they won't struggle through an illegible one. During exams it's important to write as clearly and neatly as you can, even though you are under pressure. In many schools it is expected that term papers will be handed in typed.

Learn the meaning of words. With each introductory course you take you have new words to learn, words that are used in specific ways. Make a list of these new words and their correct definition and check yourself as you use them in term papers.

Know your priorities. When you first start to college take a course plan that will be manageable. You will be spending time and energy learning how to manage your daily affairs, socializing, and taking some private time as well as going to classes. Your academic advisor will probably warn you about taking too many tough courses in the first semester and you would do well to listen. By the time the second semester rolls around, you will have learned from friends which courses are demanding, which professors to avoid, and you will be better able to build a course schedule which works for you.

Be prepared. Two of the greatest tools you can bring with you to college are the ability to type and the ability to do speed reading. You can take courses in both prior to going to college, perhaps in the last semester of your senior year when your course load is light, or over the summer. Other forms of preparation include having supplies - paper, notebooks, pens, carbon paper, a stapler, etc. - so that you're not always borrowing or having to run to the college bookstore.

Bring familiar items that make you feel "at home." Your physical comfort and sense of security can be enhanced by having old "friends" around. An added bonus is that your ease and ability to relax well can translate into better studying habits.

PROTECTING YOURSELF

"It won't happen to me."

"It won't happen to me" is a statement made by someone who has never been in an accident or emergency situation. However, once you've experienced an emergency you know it can happen again and that none of us are immune. People also define emergency differently. For our purposes, an emergency is any situation where you feel you need help right now!

The Emergency Help form lists the variety of resources that are usually available in a community. Make a copy of this form, fill in the phone numbers, and keep it posted near your telephone. If a neighbor were to pass out at your door step, or if you found your apartment had been burglarized, you would want to phone for help immediately—not search frantically for the number in the phone book or have to wait for the information operator.

Also included in this Chapter are ideas on protecting yourself in and out of your home. You may not think that anyone wants to steal your second hand television or your old furniture, but burglaries occur in all kinds of neighborhoods. And so do assaults and rape. Thoughts on how to avoid rape, as well as how to report it to the authorities, are also covered. We encourage men to read this section too, both to learn how to protect themselves from assault and to be able to be of help to a woman friend should she seek assistance after being raped. The subject of hitchhiking is discussed, but not encouraged.

Being stopped by the police and being arrested are experiences that can and do happen to law-abiding citizens. How to handle yourself should this situation occur, and knowing your legal rights are both important. Laws vary from state to state. In many states, upon reaching the age of majority (usually 18, but 21 in some states), you are considered an adult for some purposes, and a child, for others. You will want to find out what the law is with regard to where you live.

Being on your own means learning how to take care of yourself. While not a pleasant assignment, a little preparation goes a long way and you **are** worth the effort!

EMERGENCY HELP

AMBULANCE_____ **EMERGENCY HOSPITAL**_____

_____ 　_____
　　　　　　　PHONE　　　　　　　　　　　　　　　　　　　PHONE

Hospital Address_____

Directions:_____

_____

Campus Health Service:_____

Fire:_____ **Police:**_____ **Sheriff**_____

Heart Unit_____ **Crisis Line**_____

Drug Center_____ **Mental Health**_____

Rape Line_____ **Suicide Prevention**_____

Birth Control_____   **VD Hotline**_____

Pregnancy and Abortion_____

LEGAL ASSISTANCE

Attorney_____

Legal Aid Society_____

Lawyers Reference Service_____

American Civil Liberties Union (ACLU)_____

WELFARE OFFICES
Emergency Housing_____

Emergency Food_____   Foodstamp Program_____

_____   _____
PHONE   PHONE

Clothes Closet_____   Battered Women's Shelter_____

_____

Automobile Emergency Service_____

PROTECTING YOURSELF AT HOME

Assault, burglary, and rape of people while in their own home has been on the rise. Males as well as females are victims. There is no way to be 100 percent free of attack, but there are precautions that you can take to make your home and yourself more secure. It takes time, effort, money and awareness to protect yourself and your home.

— Have a bolt lock at front and rear doors.

— Keep all exterior doors and windows securely locked. Sliding glass doors should have a rod placed in the track.

— All entrances and hallways should be well lit.

— Hang curtains and/or blinds on all windows.

— Be aware of places attackers might hide, both inside and outside, or in an open garage. Trim back large shrubs outside house that would be potential hiding places. If possible, keep outside areas brightly lit.

— *NEVER* open the door to a stranger. Always ask who is at the door before opening the door. Be leary of people who claim to be from the telephone company, gas company, etc. who were not requested to come.

— Remember, many rapes are committed by assailants known to the victim.

— Women living alone or with other women should not put their full name on the mailbox or in the phone book. (Use first initial only.) Avoid publicizing that you live alone.

— Let a friend, landlord, or neighbor, know when you leave, and when you plan to return. Ask someone to collect your mail and newspaper so it is not obvious that you're alone.

Make these security precautions a daily habit — You are worth the effort.

PROTECTING YOURSELF OUTSIDE YOUR HOME

Assaults and rapes are happening in daylight as well as in the evening and night, and in so-called "good neighborhoods" and on campuses as well as in "high crime" areas. Below are several life-saving ideas for do-it-yourself crime prevention. Most importantly, remember that you are not immune to attack and that it is up to you to protect yourself.

— Walk in well lit areas. Avoid walking alone if you can.

— Walk at a steady pace, look confident and purposeful. Know where you are going. Check a map first. Don't look lost. It will draw attention to you.

— Vary your route home so that no one can plan an assault on you.

— Listen for footsteps and voices nearby. Check for someone following you. If someone is following, cross a street or walk in the middle of the street and stay near street lights.

— If you fear danger, scream loudly, yell "Fire!" Get to a lighted place fast. Run and yell.

— Carry a whistle around your wrist or on your key chain. Use it. Put your keys through your fingers as a possible sharp object.

— If you are waiting outside, stand balanced. Be suspicious of cars that pull up near you, or if a car returns and passes again and again.

— If a car is following you, turn around and walk in the reverse direction.

— Consider how you dress. If necessary, carry your dressy shoes and wear shoes good for walking and running.

— Walk near the curb, away from possible hiding places.

— Have your car key out and ready to use when you approach your parked car.

— Check the interior of your car before you get in. Always keep your car locked when you park it.

— Always carry enough money for an emergency when you go out. Have a dime taped in a convenient place in your purse or jacket pocket for an emergency phone call.

— Carry a flare in your car and a small flashlight for emergencies.

— After you raise the hood of your car as an indicator to the police that you are having car trouble, get back into your car and lock it. Do not let a stranger get into your car, even though they say they can fix it. Ask them to call the police or highway patrol for you.

— Take courses in the martial arts.

— In some states, mace is legal. Local law enforcement agencies offer courses in the proper use of mace. One must have a permit to use and carry mace.

If You Are Assaulted

All experts agree that the first thing to do if you are assaulted is to: Try to get away. If you stay calm, you will be better able to see opportunities to escape. Do not resist a person with a gun, knife or other weapon. Don't be out to win and don't fight to keep your wallet.

Crime experts do not agree whether it is best to fight back. This is a decision you need to think about for yourself. Here are two ideas for fighting back:

1. If you are attacked from behind, SCREAM!! Use the back of your head and slam it into your attacker's face; jab your elbow into his stomach; kick him in the shins; if he puts a hand over your mouth, BITE HIM; hit him with anything (handbag, tennis racket, books) you can grab.

2. If you are attacked from the front, SCREAM!! Kick him in the groin; hit him in the throat, nose, eyes, and run towards light and people.

Carry a whistle on your key chain. Always take out your keys before leaving to go to your car or house. If attacked, use your keys to scratch your attacker's face and blow your whistle loud and long!

RAPE

Being a rape victim is a traumatic experience. Rape happens to both men and women. Most people have felt such shame and anger during and after the event that they have chosen not to report the crime. In recent years, due to the enormous efforts of women's groups, police and hospital personnel are more sensitive to the medical and emotional needs of rape victims. In this new atmosphere, women have felt more encouraged to press criminal charges and to undergo the stress and sometimes the personal harassment which comes with involving themselves with the criminal justice system.

Rape is defined as unlawful carnal knowledge of a woman by force and against her will. It is up to the victim usually to give evidence of force or in some way prove that the act was against her will. Rape laws and treatment of victims of rape vary from state to state.

The most important point to remember if you are assaulted is that your life may be at stake. While it is important not to say or do anything which could be construed as consenting to the act, you must remember that the rapist may be a very sick man and that he may have a gun or other weapon. There may be situations where it is preferable to submit to the rape than to endanger your life!

If you are a rape victim, the following points are important to remember:

1. An exam must be performed within 72 hours to be accepted as proof of penetration. Semen is evidence and a shower should not be taken, nor should you wash yourself or change clothing before being examined.

2. If you go immediately to the police, they will take you for a medical exam after you give them a preliminary statement. Again, it is important to present yourself to the police in the condition in which you were left, as this is major evidence of the act of rape.

3. Your interview with the police may be easier if you bring a friend along, a counselor from your local rape crisis center, or if you ask to talk with a woman law enforcement officer.

4. Talk with the examining physician or with your private doctor about whether you should have a pregnancy test and venereal disease tests.

5. If you have a boyfriend or girlfriend, you may want to include him or her in the total process. If problems develop as a consequence of the rape, couple counseling may be helpful.

PROTECTING YOURSELF WHILE HITCHHIKING

Avoid hitchhiking whenever possible. If you don't have a car of your own, think about arranging a ride with a friend, borrowing a car, using public transportation, or joining a car pool.

If you are one of those people who will not give up hitchhiking, here are a few ideas on how to best protect yourself:

— If you're a woman, only accept rides with a woman.

— If you're a man and you accept a ride from another man, you run the risk of assault and/or rape.

— Avoid hitchhiking alone.

— Become familiar with vehicle makes, styles and colors.

— Check the license plate number before getting into the car.

— Check to see that no one is hiding in the back seat.

— Don't get into the back of a van.

— Make sure the inside handle of the passenger's side is working.

— Ask the driver's destination and determine if that is where you want to go.

— Tell the driver the cross street you want to be let out at and don't ask for a ride directly to your door.

— Don't talk too openly about yourself.

If you feel any discomfort about the situation, don't get into the car. Even though you want a ride and the person was willing to stop, you do not need to accept the offer. If you do get into a car and begin to feel uncomfortable, you may ask to be let out at a crossroad. You don't have to explain your feelings, but you do best if you trust them.

If you are the driver, it is recommended that you do not pick up hitchhikers. Many hitchhikers have been known to attack their drivers.

IF YOU ARE ARRESTED
Practical Suggestions About You and the Police

Being stopped by the police or placed under arrest is a trying experience whether or not you are guilty of violating the law. Knowing your basic rights will be helpful should this situation occur.

All citizens are guaranteed basic civil rights as written in the Bill of Rights. The laws in some states liberally interpret these rights, and you will find variations from state to state. The American Civil Liberties Union, a privately funded organization founded to defend the Bill of Rights, has available clearly written pamphlets defining the basic civil rights laws in each state. Contact your local or state ACLU office to obtain this information.

The following information is based on several states' laws and although not pertaining to all states, offers some general guidelines.

If You are Stopped for Questioning

1. You must identify yourself when a police officer asks you to do so. To avoid trouble, give your name and address or a good identification card. It is not a crime to refuse to answer further questions, although refusing to do so can make the police suspicious.

2. The police may "pat down" your clothing to check for concealed weapons. Don't physically resist. Make it verbally clear that you don't consent to any further search.

3. Ask if you are under arrest. If you are told that you are, you have a right to know why.

4. Don't "bad mouth" the police or try to run away. This is considered resisting arrest and is taken seriously.

If You are Stopped in Your Car

1. Show your driver's license and registration.

2. Your car can be searched without a warrant so long as the police have probable cause. To protect yourself later, make it verbally clear that you do not consent to the search.

3. If you are given a ticket, you should sign it. Signing means that you acknowledge receipt of the ticket, not that you agree that you violated the law.

If You Are Arrested

1. You have the right to remain silent. Tell the police nothing except

your name and address. Don't give explanations, excuses, or stories. Whatever you say can be used against you.

2. Within three hours after you are arrested, you have the right to make *two* free, completed phone calls. You may call either a lawyer, a bailbondsman, or a relative or friend. The police may not listen to the call to the lawyer.

3. Don't talk to anyone about your arrest without first talking with a lawyer. If you cannot afford a lawyer, the judge will appoint a public defender (an attorney paid by the county) to represent you.

4. You must be taken before the judge on the next court day after being arrested. At this time it will be decided whether to dismiss the case, to continue until a further date, allow you out on bail, or on your own recognizance (known as "O.R."). A lawyer will be appointed to represent you if you have not selected one yourself.

This is not complete advice! If arrested, the most important thing for you to do is to get the advice from an attorney as to how best to proceed with your case.

LEISURE AND RECREATION

TIME MANAGEMENT

All work and no play makes for a dull day . . . and week . . . and season. It also makes for a dull person, one who feels sluggish and whose work lacks spark and interest. It's important to your physical and emotional health to find a balance between work, play and rest. By play we mean physical, social and personal activities.

In order to enjoy periods of leisure it's important to manage your time well. In this section we show you how to use a Personal Energy Resource Tracer, a chart which you fill in weekly. This chart indicates when you have free time and allows you to then use that time as you need or as you choose.

We have listed a number of leisure time activities and invite you to read this list, think about what interests you, and add to it as you see fit.

It takes careful planning to keep within a budget while on vacation. We discuss vacations, why you need them, how to plan them, and when and how to best use the services of a travel agent. Included is a section on air travel, packing, passport information and tips for staying healthy while away from home.

THE PERSONAL ENERGY RESOURCE TRACER

On the following pages you will find two forms of the Personal Energy Resource Tracer: a-week-at-a-glance and the more long-range planning tracer. These charts are an efficient way for you to note and visualize all that you have to do. Once you block out all the activities that are not flexible, such as class or your work schedule, you can then see what time frames are open.

At the beginning of the week, sit down and block out the time zones for which you have definite commitments. Then, under the column for Activities, note the extra or special activities that you know need to be done during this week.

Let's say that under your activities column you have research for a term paper, reservation for going home, a birthday card for your grandmother, shoes to a repair shop, etc. Each of these tasks is not equally important but you may want to do them all. If you organize yourself, there is probably no reason why you can't. (If it looks as though it won't be humanly possible to accomplish everything, however, you may have to assign priorities.) Working from the list, you should plan on a block of time to spend researching in the library. It also looks as though you should plan a trip to a commercial area where you can buy a card, make your reservations, get your shoes repaired, etc.

Working from a PERT chart may look rigid but actually it will help you organize when you have time for relaxing and unstructured fun. Whether you are confined to a school schedule or a work schedule effective time planning can make your free hours even more enjoyable.

EFFECTIVE TIME MANAGEMENT
A Personal Checklist

1. Skim books. Read first and last paragraphs of newspaper stories.

2. Use waiting time in the office for constructive work: reading, planning or writing.

3. Keep 3x5 cards in my pocket or purse to jot down notes and ideas.

4. Keep a PERT Chart for visible time management.

5. Keep my watch a few minutes fast.

6. Put variety into my schedule by planning well in advance, leaving some time for "hot" projects and unexpected interruptions.

7. Don't procrastinate. Ask myself, "what am I avoiding?" Then face the challenge head-on.

8. Schedule the most profitable parts of a big project first. Often you won't have to do the rest.

9. Do my thinking on paper. A problem well written is half solved. Besides, good ideas can be too quickly forgotten if not preserved.

10. Work alone creatively at my best time. Use the other times for meetings, taking care of routine tasks.

11. Deal with trivia at occasional times. A three-hour session every few weeks may suffice.

12. Delegate everything I possibly can.

13. List the most important activities for the next day in order of priority, making the list at the end of the work day.

14. Designate a po.tion of my day for uninterrupted time, not taking any phone calls or visitors.

A Week-at-a-Glance

NOVEMBER	Sat. 17	Sun. 18	Mon. 19	Tues. 20	Wed. 21	Thurs. 22	Fri. 23
Morning							
Afternoon							
Evening							

Activities

Telephone calls
  travel agent for reservations
  Lee for dinner next week

Written Reports
  research—start anthro. paper
  book report for lit. 2

Meetings
  Political Club
  (Monday noon)
  Hiking Club
  (Wed. nite)

Personal Care
  hair cut
  hiking boots need resoling

Family
  grandma's birthday (Sun. 25)
  write to Sue

Social/play
  concert Sat. night
  Bowling with Bud Mon. at 5
  racket ball with Phil Wed. at 5

PERSONAL ENERGY RESOURCE TRACER

THINGS TO DO	September 13 15 20 25 30	October 1 5 10 15 20 25 30	November 1 5 10 15 20 25 30	December 1 5 10 15 20 25 30	January 1 5 10
TELEPHONE CALLS					
Call Parents about Xmas					
Friend for date		▓	▓		
Library for Info.		▓			
Travel Agent					
WRITTEN REPORTS					
Term Paper for Eng.	▓	▓	▓		
One page for Hist.	▓				
Write Thank You Notes	▓				
MEETINGS AND CONFERENCES					
Church Services	▓	▓	▓	▓	▓
"Y" Board meeting					
FAMILY RESPONSIBILITIES					
Get home for Xmas				▓	
Fix Larry's bike				▓	
PERSONAL ERRANDS					
Get shoes repaired		▓	▓		
Mail letters			▓		
TIME FOR PLAY					
Soccer practice		▓	▓	▓	

With this chart you will be able to see if you have conflicts with deadlines.

SOME LEISURE AND RECREATIONAL ACTIVITIES

The American College Dictionary defines recreation as: 1. refreshment by means of some pastime, agreeable exercise, or the like. 2. a particular form or means of such refreshment, or a pastime, diversion, exercise, or other resources affording relaxation and enjoyment. Below is a list of some recreational activities which you might like to investigate. Some activities cost money, some are done alone, some with one or more persons; some are done at home and others away; and each requires various amounts of time.

Reading for pleasure

Gardening, sewing, cooking

Auto repair

Crafts

Playing a musical instrument

Listening to music

Writing for pleasure

Photography

Book Store Browsing

Walking, jogging, running

Team Games (soccer, baseball, volleyball, etc.)

Partner Games (tennis, racket ball, ping pong, squash)

Hiking, dancing, golf, sailing, rafting, rollerskating, frisbee, swimming

Pool, billiards, cards

Sponsoring a Club (scouts, Y-Teens)

Volunteering hospital, community agency)

Discussion group with friends

Community or campus political group

Movies, theatre, T.V.

Talking with friends

Religious groups or attending services

VACATION

If we think of vacation as a time to vacate, to leave our regular daily life, we open up many possibilities. Then a vacation can mean going away, but it also can mean staying home and doing things we don't ordinarily do when we're enmeshed in a daily schedule. So, a vacation can be time to go camping, or flying to another part of the country (or the world), or it may mean staying put and reading the current best seller, eating out, visiting friends, setting up your desk for greater efficiency, sewing new clothes, painting your bedroom, gorging on movies, etc.

When you are in school, vacations come with some regularity. Of course, you may need the time to work on a large research paper and you may not have the money to vacation in a grand manner. However, it is important to your general well-being that you do plan for some periods, even short ones, that change your scene and your schedule. All work and no play not only makes you dull but also less efficient.

When you are employed you generally have two to three weeks of vacation per year. You need to find out what company policy is regarding vacation. Questions to ask include how long can you take, whether the time can be divided, how it is determined when you can go, when is the vacation schedule set, and whether you can take extra time if you're willing to forego the pay.

It is rarely possible near holidays or during the summer to decide one morning that you're off for holiday and be able to pick up the phone and make reservations for transportation and hotel. You might just luck out on someone else's bad luck and pick up their cancelled reservations but for the most part travel plans have to be made ahead . . . way ahead if you want the best choice of rooms, flight times and flight costs. This is not true for posh vacations alone, as even in national parks (and some state parks too) reservations have to be made ahead.

When planning on how you are going to use your vacation time you will want to ask yourself certain key questions?

1. **How much time do I have?**

2. **How much energy do I have?**

3. **How much money do I have for vacation?**

4. **How would I like to spend the time?**

5. **Where would I like to be go?**

6. **With whom would I like to spend my time?**

Remember, all of these questions end with the words "this year as next year your job, money, needs, time, and relationships may be different." When you first leave home it may seem quite important to return for vacations. In a few years you may feel less connected with old friends and you may be less eager to spend your time and money going home, but, at the same time you may want to visit with your parents and sibs. Think about suggesting to your family that they come visit you in your new locale or that you all meet in a new place. Do some research about what it would cost for all of you to go skiing, or camping, or renting a house by the beach somewhere.

Browsing through the travel section of your local bookstore or library will give you ideas for imaginative vacations. Universities and colleges often have tour groups at student rates. Alumni Associations, too, sponsor tours and often you don't need to be an alum. Some major universities sponsor research expeditions where you may be eligible if you're willing to work and to pay for the privilege. Unions and credit unions often offer good group rates and tours. You may not have the time or money to go on the trip of your dreams this year, but you can start planning and saving. In the meantime, be as creative as you can on how you use your timeoff. You may not have to climb the mountains of Peru, or run the Grand Canyon to refresh yourself and return to work or school with new vigor.

TRAVEL AGENTS . . . WHAT CAN I EXPECT?

If you're planning to leave Los Angeles and go home to Tulsa for Christmas vacation an airlines reservation clerk can give you information as to flight times, costs, stops, and can write your ticket for you. If, however, your Christmas gift is a $1000.00 check for you to spend this coming summer on your dream trip to South America, then it's important to find a travel agent.

If this is a trip you've been wanting for some time then it's probable that you've done some reading and roughly know some of the places you want to visit. When you contact a travel agency, ask to speak to an agent who has a familiarity with South America. Make an appointment with that person and get a sense if the agent understands what kind of experience you're looking for. Don't feel you have to stay with the first agent you talk with. This is a major investment of money and time and it's important for you to work with someone who will be responsive to you and who has a real working knowledge of the area you wish to visit. As in anything else, travel agents specialize in different parts of the world and in different kinds of holiday trips.

A good travel agent will book you the best (and least expensive if you've told him you want to travel at the lowest cost) flight, cruise or rail travel. A competent agent will know when going economy class has other costs, to your health and comfort, and will explain why you might go to second or perhaps first class for particular portions (legs) of the trip. An agent also has all the information on special fares, package deals and hotel promotions that you would not hear about on your own.

Travel agents are paid by suppliers, i.e. airlines, hotels, resorts, even restaurants, not by customers. This means there is no direct charge to you for making reservations and for giving information and advice. However, it also means that your agent will not know of, or will play down, some of the small hotels that do not pay commissions to agents.

You might on your own write to the Chamber of Commerce of the town you plan to be in and request that you be sent a listing of the lodgings available. Then it would be up to you to write individually to each place and request the date(s) you wish a room. If you are especially adventuresome you might have an agent book you a round-trip flight and a hotel for only one night; then scout out a place for the remainder of your trip.

A good travel agent wants your return business and wants you to recommend him or her to your friends. The more bookings made the more commissions earned. Thus, a good travel agent wants to do well by you so that you will return. A superb travel agent is one who calls you on your return home and asks how it went for you and what information you could give to add to his knowledge.

AIR TRAVEL INFORMATION

Air travel fares and rules are changing so rapidly that any information you have is probably out of date. To get accurate information, write or call The Civil Aeronautics Board, (CAB) Consumer Information Center, Pueblo, Colorado, 81009.

Boosts in air fares, primarily due to increased fuel costs, will probably affect all routes or airlines. Because of deregulation, there is a full menu of fares and promotional offerings. One airline may charge more for a particular trip than another. Finding the bargains means finding a travel agent who is willing to track them down for you.

Make travel plans as far ahead as possible. The number of discount seats is usually limited and the cheaper tickets are often sold out weeks ahead (months ahead for foreign travel).

If you are a student, ask about student rates. Some airlines have a number of seats so designated, others do not. Find out about "student standby" rates.

Learn what you rights are in case you are bumped, that is, if the airline has oversold. Under CAB rules, an airline which overbooks a flight must ask for volunteers who are willing to be bumped in exchange for compensation. The amount of the compensation can vary; you can sometimes bargain with the airline representative. If there are no volunteers—or if there aren't enough—the airline gets to decide who will fly. If you are bumped involuntarily, the airline must pay you the fare to your destination, up to a maximum of $200. If the airline can't arrange another flight within two hours of the original flight (four hours on international flights), the amount of compensation is doubled.

In either case you get to keep your original ticket and use it on a later flight or turn it in for a refund. Don't be put off by promises; either you fly or you get immediate compensation.

Ask your travel agent or airline reservation clerk if there will be a meal served on your flight. If you are a vegetarian or have special dietary needs requests are usually honored if advance notice is given.

Make sure you arrive for flight at least 45 minutes ahead of boarding time. This is especially important during the holiday season as airports are madhouses at that time.

If you are traveling fairly short distances you might want to check bus schedules for convenience and price, rather than always flying. By the time you reach an airport, fly, and get from the airport to the center of town, you have often spent as much time as would have been involved in going by bus. With rising air costs, bus companies are increasing their service areas. The larger bus companies such as Greyhound and Continental also have attractive travel packages wherein you go by bus, stop at resorts or urban centers for a few days, and pick up another bus to continue to your destination.

QUESTIONS TO ASK YOURSELF, YOUR TRAVEL AGENT AND YOUR GOVERNMENTAL AGENCIES WHEN PLANNING YOUR TRIP

To Your Travel Agent

When is the cheapest time to travel to _____?

What is the best price on flights that you can get for me?

Tell your travel agent you are willing to fly at odd hours.

Up to what date can I change my reservations w/o charge?

Do I need a passport, visa, health certificate, etc.?

Where can I get traveler's checks in the currency of the country I'm visiting?

How early do I need to get to the airport?

To Yourself

What am I expecting from this trip?

How do I plan on accomplishing it?

Do I want to travel alone, with a partner, in a group?

Do I want to see a lot or see one place in depth?

To the Governmental Agencies

What documents do I need for country I am visiting?

Where do I get these documents?

What if I am not a citizen of the United States?

What if I'm arrested?

What about Driver's License for renting a car?

What am I allowed to bring back from a foreign country?

What kinds of taxes are put on my purchases?

Should I register with anyone in the country I'm visiting?

TIPS ON TRAVELING

Packing

Pack light! It's expensive, exhausting and unnecessary to have bags of clothing to tote around.

Think about the weather and the kinds of events you will most likely be attending on your trip. Select outfits that have interchangeable pieces—a lot of things which mix and match well together. You may get bored wearing the same thing day after day, but nobody else will know and having manageable luggage is its own advantage.

You'll probably have one bag that you send through and a smaller one that you carry with you. In your carry-on bag or back pack, keep your toilet articles, medicine, a sweater, and important papers. If you are bringing anything of value, such as jewelry, don't ever put it in a bag that you are checking through: Carry it with you. It does happen that luggage is lost or delayed, so it is essential for you to have everything you **really** need with you. It's also a good idea to bring some dried fruit or crackers, as airports and train or bus terminals have limited services in their off-hours and are not generally known for their gourmet food during their on-hours.

Luggage Allowances

Passengers on domestic flights (U.S.) may check three pieces of luggage free of charge but no piece can weigh more than 70 pounds. The third piece is called "carry-on" and must be able to fit under your airplane seat. Purses and cameras are not counted. If you carry with extra or extra weight, you will pay extra. Charges vary, but they are usually quite high.

On foreign flights, you are allowed 66 pounds in first class and 44 pounds in economy class. While your baggage may meet the requirements of one airline, it may be considered excessive to another and you may be charged extra. Always check with the airlines you plan on using to avoid "surprises."

Traveler's Checks

Buying traveler's checks before leaving the U.S. is the best way to safeguard your money. There are two kinds of traveler's checks:

1. Destination currency traveler's checks can be bought in the U.S. at major banks in urban areas. These traveler's checks are in the currency of the country that you are going to. Destination currency checks have the double advantage of being cashed free of service charge and protecting you against loss if the exchange rate drops.

2. Traveler's checks which are bought in U.S. currency and then converted abroad in banks, stores, hotels, or restaurants. Major airports have money exchanges so that immediately upon arrival or departure you can have local currency. However, the best exchange rates are at the main offices of banks rather than at airports, in your hotel or at cheque points where the service charges are high and the exchange rates poor.

Roughing It

Many countries have excellent camping facilities, providing the cheapest and possibly most intimate way of getting to know a place. Check into this possibility.

Many families also open up their homes to students and other foreign tourists. This, too, can be a wonderful way to get to know a country.

Travel Books

At bookstores and libraries you can find a wide selection of books on how and where to travel. It's a good idea to do some reading before you go so that you know about weather, "the lay of the land," special customs, and any places you wouldn't want to miss. The Big Three of travel books, which are carefully researched on a yearly basis, are the Michelin Guide, Fodor's and travel books by Arthur Frommer.

The U.S. Government Printing Office also publishes small, easy-to-read, inexpensive, and valuable books which may be helpful to you. Travel agents and airlines often have a supply of these pamphlets. Auto Clubs are an excellent resource for trip planning, maps, routes, and tour guide books.

HEALTH TIPS FOR TRAVELERS

The biggest health risk faced by travelers is called "turista." It was thought for a long time that turista was caused by any number of things: irregular schedule, spicy foods, changes in altitude. We now know that it is the water and something in the water that causes it. Avoiding contaminated water, and foods touched by it, is quite difficult, but with some thought it can be done.

1. Do not drink tap water.

2. Never trust your hotel or restaurant manager in telling you that they have a water filter system.

3. Do not drink beverages with ice.

4. Do not eat fruits or salads which have been washed in tap water. Of course, that means only eat fruits and vegetables that have been peeled (preferably by yourself), or that have been boiled.

5. Avoid cooked foods that have been standing and are cool.

6. Drink beer or carbonated liquids in sealed bottles.

Traveling in underdeveloped areas of the world and in the tropics demand special precautions. As soon as you decide that you will be taking such a trip, talk with your physician to work out a schedule of immunizations which will fully protect you.

The U.S. Public Health Service demands that you guard yourself (and thus not contaminate your fellow country-persons) against smallpox, cholera and yellow fever. The U.S. Public Health Service publishes a booklet, "The International Certificate of Vaccination," which must be stamped by a public health agency certifying the manufacturer and lot number of the smallpox, cholera and yellow fever vaccines.

Two of the most rampant diseases in underdeveloped nations are hepatitis and venereal disease. The burden is on the traveler to protect himself or herself from these diseases.

Hepatitis - Where sanitary conditions are poor, the incidence of this viral infection is very high. Protect yourself with a gamma globulin shot prior to traveling and a booster shot every four months when you remain in an underdeveloped country. Be aware of possible fecal contaminators and make sure all meat, fish, and vegetables are well cooked. Drink local beer, tea and coffee, but not milk, water, soft drinks and avoid ice cubes.

Venereal Disease - The incidence of VD in underdeveloped countries is staggering. Talk with a doctor before your trip as to the best ways to protect yourself. Know the early signs of VD and get to a treatment source immediately.

Drugs you may wish to take with you while traveling:

Aspirin - reduces fever and an aid to alleviating headaches

Antihistamine (Chlortrimetron) helpful in reducing symptoms of allergies and relieving itching bites and rashes

Paragoric or Lomotil - anti-diarrhea agent

Dramamine - motion sickness (air or water) relief

Antibiotics (tetracycline) - use to manage intestinal infection as well as upper respiratory, sinus, ear, skin and bladder infections

You may also want to bring a thermometer, sun screen, bandages, a tweezer for splinters and a first-aid ointment.

If you wear glasses make sure to bring an extra pair or carry your current prescription.

In underdeveloped areas you will want to add to your supplies:

Analgesics (codeine) for pain

Salt tablets, insect repellent, a mosquito net

Water purification tablets (halazone)

Label all medications with both generic (common) and commercial names. Glass expands and contracts under air pressure so it is best to use plastic bottles to carry medication. Do not carry pressurized cans. They can explode in unpressurized luggage sections.

If you are under medical care, have your doctor write a report that you can carry so that a new physician can continue treatment. See if your home physician can recommend a colleague to treat you abroad. If you become ill while away, your hotel probably will have a house doctor and also a list of English-speaking physicians. You can also call the American or the British Embassy for a referral. The International Association for Medical Assistance to Travelers (IAMAT), 350 Fifth Ave., New York 10001, will provide you with a list of English-speaking doctors throughout the world. There is no charge but they would appreciate a donation with your request.

PASSPORT INFORMATION

You must have a current passport to enter all foreign countries and to re-enter the United States. You can go across the Mexican or Canadian border for less than a day without a passport. Your travel agent can tell you for which foreign countries you need a visa or other documentation.

Applications for passports can be obtained at one of the 14 Government passport agencies: in Boston, Stamford, Conn., New York City, Philadelphia, Washington, Miami, Detroit, Chicago, New Orleans, Houston, Seattle, San Francisco, Los Angeles or Honolulu. Check the appropriate telephone directory, under U.S. Government, Department of State, for the address. You can also apply at local post offices but it usually takes longer to process your application.

To obtain a passport you will need:

1. A certified copy of your birth certificate, a baptismal certificate, or record of elementary school enrollment is commonly accepted. To get a copy of your birth certificate, write to the Department of Birth Records (your state of birth) and for a small fee (usually $3.00) they will send a copy.

2. Two official passport pictures. Such pictures must be 2"x2", full-face photos, either in black or white or color and taken within the last 6 months. See your yellow pages for those photographers qualified to provide passport photos.

3. A current driver's license or current identification card from the Department of Motor Vehicles, an employment I.D., or an income tax return.

4. $14.00 (includes execution fee), paid in check or money order.

If you plan on doing much traveling request a 48 or 96 page passport. There is no extra charge for the larger size.

A passport is valid for five (5) years.

If you change your name you must make the change officially on your passport by notifying the U.S. Passport Agency.

To renew your passport, you need:

1. a passport renewal form available at your local post office.

2. two current passport pictures

3. $10.00 renewal charge, in check or money order.

Send the above, along with your old passport, to the U.S. Passport Agency whose address is on the renewal form.

In your address book or somewhere safe, keep the passport number and the date of issue. Then, if your passport is lost or stolen you can more readily speed the replacement process.

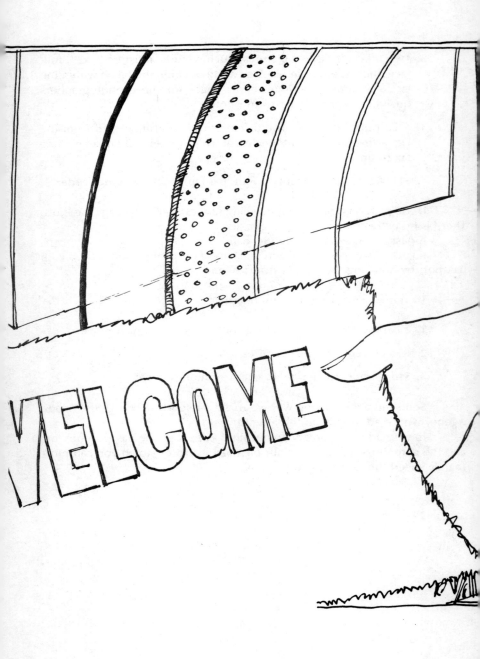

YOU CAN GO HOME AGAIN

In his great American novel, *You Can't Go Home Again,* Thomas Wolfe describes a young man's disappointment and confusion when he returns to his old home and finds himself uncomfortable and out of tune with his old environment. It's understandable and a common condition if you, too, find yourself in varying degrees of confusion and discomfort when you return home. After all, your family has adjusted and adapted to losing one of its members, just as you have adjusted and adapted to being away.

The first step toward easing some of this discomfort is to acknowledge the changes that have been made. Perhaps you and your family will decide that when you're home, you will pick up where you left off, such as doing your old chores. Or you may all agree that when you're home you will do some of the more unusual work, such as cleaning out the garage or doing more of the cooking. In some cases, returning family members are treated as welcome house guests without any responsibilities for household duties. Talk about it.

While living on your own, you probably don't have to let anyone know where you've gone or when you expect to return, even though it's always a safety precaution. In most homes, it's a matter of common courtesy that family members give such information so that plans can be made. If you look at this as a courtesy rather than a demand or restriction, you will probably have less trouble complying. Hopefully, your parents recognize your new status and growth and will be better able to be less "parental" as they see you as an adult.

Each family differs in its family rules such as curfew, bedtime, drinking, smoking, and guests during the day, evening, mealtime, or overnight. Don't take anything for granted. Check out with your parents how they feel about these things. Oftentimes what was permissible when you were a minor is not OK with them when you are an adult. They may not want to give you an allowance, pocket money or see you lounging around the house.

You and your family should recognize that you have all changed a little—maybe a lot—and that a family conference may be necessary in helping all of you through the re-entry process. You may need to be the one to initiate this new balance by speaking to your parents individually or together, conferring with your siblings or—even more effective—calling for a family meeting.

IV. ROOTS AND RECORDS

PERSONAL JOURNAL PAGES

YOUR PERSONAL RECORD KEEPER

Your Personal Record Keeper is a data bank about you and your family. Once these forms are completed, you will have a permanent record about your birth, medical, educational and religious history, as well as a three-generational family history. You will need some of this information to fill out job, school and passport applications; you will want some of it as you try to piece together events in life—What year did I break my leg?—and as you watch your own children develop.

Medical science tells us how important it is to know about the major diseases and causes of death of our blood relatives. Given this information, your doctor may be better able to design a preventive health program specifically for you. Hopefully, after you leave home, you will start your own health and medical care record. A form indicating your current insurance coverage is also included.

We all know that ignorance is not bliss. We have included a form for parents so that in the event of a catastrophic illness or death, their business and legal affairs can be managed and their professional representatives easily located. It is up to parents and young adults to continue to keep this form up to date.

So that you can keep in touch with favorite friends and relatives, we have included a form wherein you can jot down not only the address, but the person's birthday or anniversary. There is another form which makes it easy for you to buy them gifts that fit!

This chapter demands time and attention in order that the forms can be filled in as completely and accurately as possible. We believe it will be a rewarding and loving experience for a parent and child leaving home to work on this together.

YOUR BIRTH INFORMATION

Birthday_____
        (day of the week)   (month)   (day)   (year)

Birth time_____Birth weight_____length_____

Doctor in attendance_____

Hospital or other place of birth_____

        City and State_____

Method of childbirth: Natural_____Lamaze_____Leboyer_____

Saddleblock_____Caesarean_____Other_____

Complications of pregnancy and/or delivery:

_____

_____

Drugs mother took during pregnancy:

_____

_____

Christened: Where_____Date_____

Godparents:_____

Circumcision information: Where_____

                            By whom_____

Other information about your birth:_____

_____

_____

_____

_____

FAMILY HISTORY — Paternal Side

(Father's Full Name)

Born:_____Where:_____

Died:_____Where:_____

Education:_____

(Name of school)   (dates)   (degree)   (major)

Married: _____
         (date)   (to whom)   (where)

         _____
         (date)   (to whom)   (where)

Divorced:
Widowed: _____
         (date)   (where)

Occupation: (major jobs held)

Dates: _____
         (from   to   )   (employer)

         (from   to   )   (employer)

         (from   to   )   (employer)

         (from   to   )   (employer)

Military Service:_____
         (branch of service)   (where served)

Special awards, medals, etc.

Special interests or important events:

Children: (listed in birth order)

     Date:_____

     _____

FAMILY HISTORY — Paternal Side (continued)

grandmother		grandfather
_____	born (date)	_____
_____	Where	_____
_____	Died (date)	_____
_____	Education	_____
_____	Occupation	_____
_____	Married	_____
_____	Divorced	_____

Children (listed in birth order)
date of birth

_____   _____

_____   _____

_____   _____

_____   _____

_____   _____

_____   _____

Other information regarding paternal grandparents:

FAMILY HISTORY — Maternal Side

_____
(Mother's Full Name)

Born:_____Where:_____

Died:_____Where:_____

Education:_____

_____
(Name of school)   (dates)   (degree)   (major)

_____

_____

Married: _____
              (date)   (to whom)   (where)

_____
              (date)   (to whom)   (where)

Divorced:
Widowed: _____
              (date)   (where)

Occupation: (major jobs held)

Dates: _____
              (from   to   )   (employer)

_____
              (from   to   )   (employer)

_____
              (from   to   )   (employer)

_____
              (from   to   )   (employer)

Military Service:_____
                        (branch of service)   (where served)

_____
        Special awards, medals, etc.

Special interests or important events:

Children: (listed in birth order)

        Date:_____

_____

FAMILY HISTORY — Maternal Side (continued)

grandmother		grandfather
	born (date)	
	Where	
	Died (date)	
	Education	
	Occupation	
	Married	
	Divorced	

Children (listed in birth order)
date of birth

Other information regarding maternal grandparents:

RELIGIOUS RECORD

Father's religion:_____

Mother's religion:_____

Church/Temple attended by family:

_____
(name)   (location)

              _____
                        (name of leader)

_____
(name)   (location)

              _____
                        (name of leader)

_____
(name)   (location)

              _____
                        (name of leader)

Dates and special memories of these events:

Baptized:_____

First Communion:_____

Bar Mitzva/Bat Mitzva:_____

Confirmation:_____

Wedding:_____

Other Religious Ceremonies:_____

SCHOOL HISTORY

Elementary Schools Attended:

_____
(name)   (address)   (city)   (dates)

_____
                                                                            (dates)

Special Awards:_____

Junior High Schools attended:_____

_____
                                                                            (dates)

Special Awards:_____   _____

High Schools attended:_____
                                                                            (dates)

_____
                                                                            (dates)

Diploma_____ Date   GED_____ (date)_____

High School Proficiency_____(date)_____

High School Teachers who would recommend me:

_____ School_____

_____ School_____

Colleges attended:

_____
                                                                            (date)

_____
                                                                            (date)

Special Awards:_____

Degrees:_____
                                                                            (Major)

Professors who would recommend me:

_____ College_____

_____   _____

HEALTH RECORD

Dental History:

Information on baby teeth (when teeth came in, complications)

_____

Information on permanent teeth (cavities, broken teeth, etc.

_____

Orthodontic Treatment: Work started_____Work comp._____

Comments:_____

_____

Dentist_____ Orthodontist_____

Address_____ Address_____

Phone_____ Phone_____

Eye History:

Visual impairment noted at age _____ Type_____

Treatment_____

Eye Surgery: Year_____ Correction: Yes____ No____ 0 Partial____

Eye Surgeon:_____Hospital_____

Prescription for corrective lens/contact lenses:

First prescription:_____Most recent prescription_____
                        (date)   (date)

Name of Optometrist:_____Phone_____

Address:_____

Comments:_____

Mental Health History:

Problems:_____

Year   Therapist/Clinic   Treatment

- _____

Psychological Testing:

Year   **Psychologist**   **Name/Address of Clinic**

_____

_____

_____

_____

_____

Accidents/Broken Bones:

Year   Break   Clinician's name and address

_____

_____

_____

X-Rays and Special Studies:

Year   Section of Body   Clinician's name and address

_____

_____

_____

Hospitalization

Year   Procedure   Clinician's name and address

            Appendectomy

_____

            Tonsilectomy/
            Adnoidectomy

_____

_____

_____

Allergies:

Year	Allergic Agent	Reaction/Symptom	Treatment

Allergist: Name:_____   Address:_____

_____

_____

HEALTH RECORD

Blood Type_____   Rh Factor_____

Record of Childhood Illnesses

Year	Illness	Year	Illness
_____	Chicken Pox	_____	Sinusitis
_____	Measles	_____	Tonsilitis
_____	German Measles	_____	Tuberculosis
_____	Mumps	_____	Glandular Disease
_____	Whooping Cough	_____	Pneumonia
_____	Scarlet Fever	_____	Bronchitis
_____	Diptheria	_____	Influenza
_____	Roseola infantum	_____	Appendicitis
_____	Urinary Infection	_____	Rheumatic Fever
_____	Poliomyelitis	_____	Skin diseases
_____		_____	Other:

Immunization Record

Polio 1_____Polio 2_____Polio 3_____Polio Booster_____

Measles_____Mumps_____Rubella_____Tetanus Booster_____

Other Immunizations:

_____ _____ _____ _____

Tests and Special Examinations

Schick Test

Year_____

Reaction_____

Clinician_____

Audiogram

Year_____

Reaction_____

Clinician_____

Tuberculin

Year_____

Reaction_____

Clinician_____

Gynecological

Year_____

Reaction_____

Clinician_____

If medical specialists were consulted regarding the above, list names and addresses on a blank page.

FAMILY HEALTH HISTORY

Relative	Birthdate	Major Health Problems	Age At Time of Death	Cause
Maternal Grandmother				
Maternal Grandfather				
Paternal Grandmother				

Paternal
Grandfather

_____

Mother

_____

Father

_____

Brothers/
Sisters

_____

_____

_____

_____

_____

_____

_____

IMPORTANT FAMILY INFORMATION

(for the parent)

The hospitalization or death of a family member is a highly stressful event for the rest of the family. Eliminate some of the fear, worry and expenses children may bear during this time by carefully recording and keeping current the information on the following pages.

This information provides your son or daughter with an easily understood record of what and where your assets are to be found and lists your professional representatives.

It is important for every adult to have a last will and testament which provides for the disposition of your personal property. Without a will, your estate (small as it may be) will go through a probate court procedure, during which time any outstanding debts and burial costs must be borne by the family until access to the estate's assets can be obtained. Going through probate means expensive legal fees which then leave less in your estate for your family. Having an attorney draw up a will is usually an inexpensive legal service. It is suggested that you make several copies of this form. At least yearly, perhaps on a birthday or other significant anniversary, review and update the information and send a revised form to your children. Even, or especially, if your children protest that you are being morbid or silly, they will greatly appreciate your thoughtfulness when the time comes.

PARENTS' LEGAL AND PERSONAL DOCUMENTS

In case of accident and/or our death, please notify:

Doctor: _____   Phone_____

_____

Lawyer: _____   Phone_____

_____

Our Wills are located_____

Our Safe Deposit Box is at_____ and the keys

are_____. Funeral and cemetery arrangements

have been made with_____.

Insurance Agent_____ Phone_____

_____

Accountant_____ Phone_____

_____

Insurance_____
               (company name)   (policy #)   (Type of Ins.)

_____

_____

Social Security Numbers: _____ _____
                      Mother's   Father's

Bank Accounts:

_____
(Name of Bank)   Branch Address   Account #

_____

_____

Pension Plan
Mother's_____
        (Name of fund)   Number

Father's_____

This information is accurate as of_____
                   (Date)

IMPORTANT PEOPLE IN MY LIFE

Name

Address

Phone

Birthday/
Anniversary

January

February

March

April

May

June

July

August

IMPORTANT PEOPLE IN MY LIFE

September_____

October_____

November_____

December_____

GIFT AID

Person	Blouse	Dress	Shirt neck - sleeve	Pants waist - length	Ring

MY INSURANCE COVERAGE

Type	Insurance Company Agent's name & address	Policy No.	Coverage from/til

HEALTH
covers:

AUTO
covers:

PROPERTY
covers:

LIFE
covers:

You may be covered under your parents' policies even though you are out of their home. Check this out.

This information is accurate as of _____ _____
(date)

EPILOGUE

We hope that your First Time Out was enriched by the suggestions that were helpful to our own children, and that your return trips home are as joyful and stress-free as possible.

We would like to hear from you. Any ideas you may have for updating this book would be most welcome. Your ideas and experiences may help ease another person's First Time Out. Send your input to our publisher: Jalmar Press, Inc., 6501 Elvas Avenue, Sacramento, California 95819. Attention to Reva Camiel and/or Hila Michaelsen.

BIBLIOGRAPHY

MONEY MATTERS

Hayes, Mary Anne, *Ask the Coupon Queen,* Pocket Books, New York, 1979

Myerson, Bess, *The Complete Consumer Book: How to Buy Wisely and Well,* Simon and Schuster, New York, 1979

Newman, Stephan and Nancy, *Getting What You Deserve: A Handbook for the Assertive Consumer,* Dolphin Books, New York, 1975

Porter, Sylvia, *The Money Book,* Doubleday, New York, 1980

Center for Science in the Public Library: 99 Ways to a Simple Lifestyle, Anchor Books, New York, 1979

"Consumer Reports," Consumer's Buying Guide, published annually

HOUSING

Liles, Marcia and Robert, *Good Housekeeping Guide to Fixing Things Around the House,* Pocket Books, New York, 1976

Moskovitz, *Tenant's Rights,* Nolo Press. Occidental, California, 1977

Slater, Charlotte, *All the Things Your Mother Never Taught You,* Ballantine, New York, 1978

FOOD

Cunningham, Marion and Laber, Jeri, *The Fannie Farmer Cookbook,* Alfred A. Knopf, New York, 1979

Doyle, Rodger, *The Vegetarian Handbook,* Crown Publishers, New York, 1979

Hewitt, Jean, *The New York Times Natural Foods Cookbook,* Avon, New York, 1979

Kraus, Barbara, *Dictionary of Protein,* Harper's Magazine Press, New York, 1979

Lappe, Frances Moore, *Diet for a Small Planet,* Ballantine, New York, 1977

Rombauer, Irma and Becker, Marion Rombauer, *Joy of Cooking,* Bantam, New York, 1976

Better Homes and Gardens New Cookbook, Bantam, New York, 1976

CLOTHING

Cho, Emily and Grover, Linda, *Looking Terrific,* Ballantine, New York, 1978

Hix, Charles and Burdine, Brian, *Dressing Right,* St. Martin's Press, New York, 1978

Molloy, John T., *Dress for Success,* Warner Books, New York, 1975

BUYING A CAR

The Family Car, the Editors of Time-Life Books, Rand McNally and Company, Skokie, Illinois, 1975

Schultz, Mort, *How To Fix It: A Systematic Guide to Home, Car and Boat Repairs,* McGraw-Hill, New York, 1978

Troise, Joe, *Cherries and Lemons: The Used Car Buyer's Handbook,* And Books, 1979

PERSONAL RELATIONS

Alberti, Albert E., and Emmons, Michael L., *Your Perfect Right: A Guide to Assertive Behavior,* Impact Publishers, San Luis Obispo, California, 1978

Goldstein, Martin, M. D.,; Halberle, Edwin J.; McBride, Will, *The Sex Book: A Modern Pictorial Encyclopedia,* Bantam Books, New York, 1979

Halpern, Howard M., *Cutting Loose,* Bantam Books, New York, 1978

James, Muriel, *Marriage Is For Loving,* Addison-Wesley, Reading, Massachusetts, 1979

James and Jongeward, *Born to Win,* Addison-Wesley, Reading, Massachusetts, 1973

Landers, Ann, *Encyclopedia From A - Z (Improve Your Life Emotionally, Medically, Sexually, Socially, Spiritually)* Ballantine Books, New York, 1978

Powell, Barbara, *Overcoming Shyness,* McGraw-Hill Book Company, New York, 1979

Satir, Virginia, *Peoplemaking,* Science and Behavior Books, Palo Alto, California, 1972

Tripp, C. A., *The Homosexual Matrix,* Signet Books, New York, 1978

Underwood, Betty, and Scharff, Barbara Underwood, *Hostage to Heaven*, Clarkson N. Potter Publishing Company, New York, 1979

HEALTH

Berkeley Holistic Health Center, *Holistic Health Book*, And/Or Press, 1978

Boston Women's Collective, *Our Bodies, Ourselves*, Simon and Schuster, New York, 1977

Graedon, Joe, *The People's Pharmacy*, Avon, New York, 1976

Julty, Sam, *Men's Bodies, Men's Selves*, Dell, New York, 1979

McGuire, *The Tooth Trip*, Random House, New York, 1978

Millman, Dan, *Whole Body Fitness*, Clarkson N. Potter, New York, 1979

Vickery, Donald, and Fries, James F., *Take Care of Yourself: A Consumer's Guide to Medical Care*, Addison-Wesley, Reading, Massachusetts, 1976

CAREERS

Bolles, Richard Nelson, *What Color Is Your Parachute?, A Practical Manual for Job Hunters and Career Changers*, Ten Speed Press, Berkeley, California, 1979 rev. ed. ($5.95)

_____, *The Three Boxes of Life: And How to Get Out of Them*, Ten Speed Press, Berkeley, California, 1978

Douglas, Martha, *How To Get Your First Good Job*, Chronicle Books, San Francisco, 1979

Gale, Linda and Barry, *The National Career Directory: An Occupational Information Handbook*, Arco Publishing Company, New York, 1979

Lederer, Muriel, *Blue Collar Jobs for Women*, E. P. Dutton, New York, 1979

Mitchell, Joyce Slayton, *The Men's Career Book: Work and Life Planning for a New Age*, Bantam, New York, 1979

Ruddick, Sara and Daniels, Pamela, *Working It Out: 23 Writers, Artists, Scientists, and Scholars Talk About Their Lives and Work*, Pantheon Books, New York, 1977

Terkel, Studs, *Working*, Avon, New York, 1972

COLLEGE

Edelhart, Michael, *College Knowledge: Everything You Need to Know About Everything*, Anchor Press, New York, 1979

Eskow, Seymour, *Barron's Guide to the Two-Year College*, Barron's Educational Series, Woodbury, New York

Fine, Benjamin, *Profiles of American Colleges*, Barron's Educational Series, Woodbury, New York

Freede, S. Robert, *Cash for College*, Prentice-Hall, New Jersey, 1978

Gross, Michee J., *The How To Go To College Book*, Passage Publishers, Seattle, Washington, 1978

Moll, Richard, *Playing the Private College Admissions Game*, Times Books, New York, 1979

Morehead, Albert H., *Roget's College Thesaurus,* Grosset and Dunlop, New York, 1979

Strunck, William, and White, E. B., *The Elements of Style,* Macmillan, New York, 1979

Tobias, Shiela, *Overcoming Math Anxiety,* W. W. Norton, New York, 1978

Turabian, Kate I., *A Manual for Writers of Term Papers, Theses and Dissertations,* The University of Chicago Press, 1973

Weigan, George, *How to Succeed in High School and Score High on College Entrance Examinations,* Barron's Educational Services, Woodbury, New York, 1978

The Random House Dictionary, Random House, New York, 1980

PROTECTING YOURSELF

Brownmiller, Susan, *Against Our Will: Men, Women and Rape,* Bantam Books, New York, 1979

Media, Andra and Thompson, Kathleen, *Against Rape,* Noonday Press, New York, 1974

Nelson and Hall, *Fear Into Anger: A Manual of Self-Defense for Women,* 1978

Sussman, Alan N., *The Rights of Young People: An American Civil Liberties Handbook,* Avon, New York, 1977

TIME MANAGEMENT, LEISURE AND RECREATION

Allen, Joseph, *The Leisure Alternative Catalog,* Delta Special/Publisher's Inc., New York, 1978

Diagram Group, *Rules of the Game,* Bantam Books, New York, 1979

Fluegelman, Andrew, *The New Games Book,* Dolphin Books/Doubleday, New York, 1979

Norbert, Craig and Peter, *The New American Guide to Athletics Sports and Recreation,* Plume Books, New York, 1979

ROOTS AND RECORDS

Hilton, Suzanne, *Who Do You Think You Are? Digging for Your Family Roots,* Signet, New York, 1978

Strykr-Rodda, Harriet, *How To Climb Your Family Tree, Geneology for Beginners,* J. B. Lippincott, New York, 1977

INDEX

JOURNAL